Governance and Ministry
Rethinking Board Leadership

Governance and Ministry
Rethinking Board Leadership

DAN HOTCHKISS

THE
ALBAN
INSTITUTE

Herndon, Virginia
www.alban.org

The Alban Institute
2121 Cooperative Way, Suite 100
Herndon, VA 20171

Unless otherwise noted, all Scripture quotations are from the King James Version of the Bible.

Portions of this book have appeared in the "Faithful Finance" section of the *Clergy Journal*, published by Logos Productions, Inc. (www.logosproductions. com).

The following have given permission to reprint policy language in Appendix B: Kaleo Church, San Diego, California; St. Peter's United Church of Christ, Carmel, Indiana; Unitarian Universalist Church of Greater Lynn, Swampscott, Massachusetts; Beth El Synagogue Talmud Torah, Omaha, Nebraska; Centenary United Methodist Church, Winston-Salem, North Carolina; St. Timothy's Episcopal Church, Herndon, Virginia; McLean Bible Church, McLean, Virginia; The Union for Reform Judaism, Joint Commission on Synagogue Management, New York, New York.

Cover design by Spark Design.

Library of Congress Cataloging-in-Publication Data

Hotchkiss, Dan.
    Governance and ministry : rethinking board leadership / Dan Hotchkiss.
    p. cm.
Includes bibliographical references.
ISBN 978-1-56699-370-8
1. Church polity. 2. Church committees. 3. Christian leadership.
    4. Church management. 5. Church officers. I. Title.
BV650.3.H68 2008
254—dc22
                                2009003718

        13   12   11   10   VP   5   4   3

Contents

Foreword

Governance and ministry ... the two are joined inextricably. Vital and vibrant ministry depends on effective governance and leadership to such a great extent. Leadership and governance must be rooted in ministry and mission if they are to be more than perfunctory and technical in their scope. Recent research into congregational life makes it clear: the quality and commitment of leadership, both lay and clergy, have a direct effect on the effectiveness and growth of a local congregation.

Boards are at the very heart of good governance and leadership for a congregation. They may be called councils, sessions, vestries, or by other names, but their purpose is essential to congregational life. These groups of leaders define the mission of a congregation, assess the context in which the congregation pursues its mission, develop resources for ministry (faith, human, and financial), envision the future, and prepare strategies for ministry in the present and in the future. It is a sacred task to offer leadership as a member of a congregation's board (or boards of other religious organizations, for that matter.) God equips and empowers people for this service, as God has equipped and empowered leaders through the generations. Boards and their members make a great difference for the good, and they contribute in significant measure to a congregation's capacity to engage God's mission in a particular time and place.

All this being said, creative and capable board leadership does not occur without intent and planning. That is precisely what Dan

Hotchkiss's writing is about. Leadership needs to be developed, and governance needs to be examined, structured, and planned. Too often in congregational life, boards are left to tend themselves. The structures and patterns of governance are simply allowed to be what they always have been. Organizations and even their meeting agendas remain static and unexamined.

Dan Hotchkiss has a different vision of governance and its leadership, a vision that is dynamic, organic, and alive. He calls this leadership "an expressive art," and so it is. It is an expression of the values and commitments that are at the center of the life and identity of a given congregation. It is an art with all of the inspiration and vision associated with a creative art.

Both governance and congregational ministry and mission are being pursued today in a time of vast and fast-moving change. Former assumptions about culture and religion simply do not apply in our day and age. This places added burden and opportunity on the leaders of congregations. The burden is that things cannot be done as they once were done. Too much has changed. The culture is increasingly multiform and multiethnic. The expectations and dispositions toward religious life and institutions are radically different. The burden is that of reading the culture accurately and devising new ways of proclaiming the message and invitation to faith. The opportunity is the mirror image of the burden; it is to approach congregational mission in new ways, with a new eye to purpose, to potential, and to the populations around us.

Governance, leadership, boards, and clergy and lay leaders bear the responsibility and the opportunity for the movement of mission and congregational life into the future. This requires caring and competence from the human beings who serve in this way. They must care for the congregation and the mission it pursues with real heart, and they must bring competence in areas of strategy, planning, program, and operations. Dan Hotchkiss offers clear analysis of structures for governance and leadership and of ways that can and do work to enhance leadership and mission. He recognizes that leadership is an all-hands-on-deck pursuit today, with laity and clergy working closely and collaboratively for vision and implementation of mission. And he recognizes that the primary issue is mission—the call, purpose, and identity of congregation. When he addresses the fiduciary and "ownership" question of a congregation, he says clearly and accurately, "The 'owner' that the board must serve is this congregation's mission, the small piece of God's will that belongs to it."

Congregations are the primary communal expression of American religious life. There are other religious institutions, to be sure, and there are other "manifestations" of religious organization (judicatories, dioceses, denominations) that bind local communities of faith together and serve as resources to local congregations. But the primary expression remains the local congregation. The hundreds of thousands of congregations in this country are served and led by boards—groups of servant leaders who do the work of governance, mission development, and shaping for the future. It is imperative that prayer, thought, and intent be given to how these boards do their work and pursue their tasks. Leadership itself must be developed just as the mission of the local congregation must be developed.

It is an urgent moment for congregations and their boards. The change that is around us and within the religious world itself necessitates a new way of approaching things. Congregations must learn to be more inviting, more engaging with the culture around them, more creative and intentional in proclamation and invitation, more transparent in compassion and servanthood. It is a tall order. It is an urgent time, and it is all the more urgent for the boards of congregations. They have the responsibility and opportunity to take new approaches, govern and lead effectively, take some reasoned and inspired risks, strengthen the sense of mission, and envision and plan a new future. They... you... are uniquely in the place and position to do this work in God's name and power. To do this, boards need to address all of the things considered in this book: mission, vision, partnerships, boundaries, organization, and development.

To serve on the board of a local congregation is a sacred trust. It is to hold sacred things in trust. This is a dynamic and divine undertaking. It is dynamic in the breadth and depth of action involved in this leadership. It is divine because it is an expression of God's mission and activity embodied in the work of leading a community of faith. It is as old as Moses and the elders on their Exodus sojourn and as new as the mission and sojourn of your own congregation. The invitation to readers of this writing is to commit themselves anew to mission and leadership, to bring their caring and competence to bear, and to shape and develop the local congregation for its journey and call of mission.

James B. Lemler

Preface

Once upon a time, Americans joined congregations in the secret hope that one day someone might ask them to serve on a committee. Today that rarely happens. In fact, many of our most vital congregations now lure members by boasting about their *lack* of tedious "church work" and baroque organizational structure. They recruit, equip, and deploy people into lives of faith and service, not into committees. These new-style churches, synagogues, temples, sanghas, and mosques have discovered something that should have surprised no one: a congregation that invites people to participate in organizational life appeals to only a few, but a congregation that invites people directly into spiritual growth and service appeals to many. The result, among the fastest-growing congregations and their imitators, has been a movement to reduce bureaucracy to make room for ministry.

In such a time, it might seem odd to write or read a book on congregational governance. As an Alban Institute consultant, I have worked with congregations that grew rapidly while streamlining their decision-making process, and with others that tried to maintain scores of committees while their membership declined from thousands to hundreds to scant dozens. In time, I started to suspect that outdated, overcomplex and inward-focused structures might be one cause of decline in congregations. As I watched more systematically, I came to believe that often-mentioned trends like "the decline of the Protestant mainline" might have as much to do with governance as with theology. Growing congregations often are the ones that have reformed their structures for governance and ministry, whether they are liberal or conservative in their theology. Even more strikingly, declining congregations across the theological spectrum often share specific organizational patterns. I think those patterns are one factor in their decline—a factor, unlike social and cultural trends, that a congregation can control.

My interest in governance stems from my consulting work with congregations in strategic planning. I work with boards and planning teams to frame critical questions and to engage the congregation and its leaders in a "holy conversation." Planners gather data, pray, and prod boards and congregations to take a fresh look at persistent issues. At last, the team produces its report. Many such reports are timid or routine, but occasionally a planning document expresses a compelling vision of the future seriously different from the past.

Such cases remind me of a question Lyle Schaller, one of the pioneers of church consulting, likes to ask: "What if it works?"

When planning works, the congregation has to face what I now call the Governance Question: "What is our process for deciding to make a major change, empowering people to make it happen, and holding them accountable for the results?" Too few congregations, I find, have an adequate answer to this question, and the result, sometimes, is a beautiful planning document that makes no difference in the congregation's life.

"OK," I sometimes ask, "when was the last time you decided on and implemented a major change, a significant departure from old patterns in your congregation's life?" Generally, a silence follows, then discussion, with one of the following outcomes:

- No one can remember any major changes.
- The most recent major change happened in 1958, or 1859, or 1598.
- The most recent major change happened because people worked *around* the congregation's system of decision mak-

ing, rather than *through* it. If they had asked permission, the answer would have been no.

At some point, I began to ask the Governance Question at the beginning of the planning process rather than at the end. When I did, planning teams and governing boards often chose to make their governance structure a central focus of strategic planning. Governance reform became an important part of my consulting practice. Congregations started calling me because they had heard that I knew something about governance. They asked, "Is there a book we can read?" and I had to say, "Not yet."

There is no shortage of resources for boards. Every denomination has books and training guides, each of which has merit. But inevitably such resources, even when they are not literally "written by committee," reflect common practice as it stands more than they try to lead it. Many, many books written for business people have value for religious leaders, but it is not always easy to translate what is of value while screening out what does not fit. Most guides to business leadership focus exclusively on management, all but ignoring the role of stockholders and boards. Some congregational boards—like many corporate boards—gladly hand all power to the clergy leader, intervening only at moments of disaster, scandal, or transition. Most congregations, though, wish as a matter of principle to balance clergy leadership with lay control, and find the business-oriented literature only a partial help.

Another family of resources seeks to emphasize and cultivate a sense of the unique character of congregational boards. Charles M. Olsen, in *Transforming Church Boards into Communities of Spiritual Leaders* (Alban Institute, 1995), proposed that boards engage in narrative reflection, Scripture study, prayerful discernment, and "visioning" (a word so new in 1995 that it needed to be put between quotation marks!). Olsen's book has had wide influence and has inspired many other resources for helping boards to understand themselves as religious and not simply business leaders. As valuable as these resources have been, most of them neglect key questions: What is the board's exact role? What does it contribute to the organization? How does the board's job relate to the job of clergy, staff, committees, and the congregation? While no one answer will fit every case, a board without a clear sense of its specific role cannot resist the gravitational pull that can drag a community of spiritual leaders back to behaving as a business board. The spiritual emphasis, while essential, needs the protection that only a clear sense of institutional roles and boundaries can provide; otherwise, under pressure, boards revert to more familiar styles of operation.

Sophistication about the role of boards has evolved greatly in the nonprofit world. A wide variety of resources about board governance has become available to help with strategic planning, staff oversight, policymaking, and keeping the focus on top-level governance while staying out of management. But the work of secular thinkers like John Carver, Richard Chait, and Frances Hesselbein, and resource groups like BoardSource and the Leader to Leader Institute have barely begun to penetrate the world of congregations. One of the goals of this book is to translate some of this excellent work and make it more accessible to religious leaders.

An experience from outside my work with congregations prompted me to think about what a helpful book on congregational governance might say. Several years ago, I had an opportunity to volunteer for my son's high school. The principal had heard that I knew something about fundraising and asked me to help write some grant proposals. I said yes. Soon I got a call inviting me to attend the next meeting of the fundraising committee. I resisted—in my work I get to go to plenty of committee meetings—but finally relented. The chair assured me, "We'll talk at the meeting about what kinds of grants we want to apply for, and from there on you'll be working on your own."

I drove an hour and a half and sat with the committee. It was a pleasure to meet some of the most committed parents in the school. The doughnuts were particularly tasty. We never did talk about grants, though, because we were too busy stuffing, sealing, and addressing envelopes for the fall fundraising appeal.

If someone had asked me to stuff envelopes, I like to think I would have done it. But to find myself stuffing envelopes when I had expected to be helping make important policy decisions made me feel that I'd been involved in a game of bait and switch; the experience left me less trustful and less motivated to step forward the next time. I think I would have felt the same way had I showed up to stuff envelopes and found myself dragooned into a meeting about grant proposals.

After a while, I realized that I had just experienced, from below, the kind of volunteer experience I had inflicted on too many others. As a minister and congregational consultant, I had taken it for granted that "committees" should make most of the decisions and also do most of the work in a congregation. It had never occurred to me that people might want to make decisions *or* do work, but not both. The result, I now saw, was to frustrate and repel many of the volunteers who could accomplish the most, whether as workers or as decision makers.

At about that time I happened to meet Sharon, who told me about a different kind of volunteer experience. Someone had recruited her to work for Habitat for Humanity. Overcoming considerable reluctance, Sharon volunteered for a house-building shift. Her first construction work assignments were straightforward: measuring and marking, laying boards in place, and even—after she had returned to volunteer a few more times—swinging a hammer, Jimmy Carter–style. Sharon became a Habitat crew leader, and in time even led a team to Romania to build houses there.

Here is what amazed me about Sharon's story: she did all of this *without attending a single committee meeting!* She attended training workshops and led workshops for her crew, but at no time did she sit around a table to debate and vote on whether to build houses, where to build them, what color to paint them, or how much money they should cost. No doubt *someone* did these things—Habitat does have a board, and no doubt committees too—but it manages to offer a wide range of opportunities for people who simply want to build a house for somebody who needs a house.

These three experiences—my client congregations' difficulty implementing their strategic plans, my annoyance as a would-be grant writer stuffing envelopes, and Sharon's success as a Habitat house builder building houses—frame the beginnings of my interest in governance for congregations.

This book responds to a strong wish from leaders of congregations for tools and a road map for considering and implementing changes in the way boards and clergy work together to lead congregations. I created this material mostly for and with congregations and their leaders, but other organizations have found the ideas useful, too. Congregations have a lot to learn from progress in the rest of the nonprofit sector, and something to teach as well. The particular ideas I present here should be of interest to any organization that has some or all of the following traits in common with most congregations:

- A mission rooted in the founders' deepest values and convictions.
- An empowered constituency of people who identify passionately with the organization and its mission.
- Stakeholder groups that overlap, making it hard to draw crisp lines between management, staff, clients, donors, members, and the public.
- Leaders who think of themselves primarily as members of a profession rather than as managers.

A great many nonprofits, businesses, and governmental agencies share some or all of these characteristics and would benefit from some of the lessons congregational leaders are learning about how to govern and manage themselves.

My consulting clients deserve a lot of credit for alerting me to the widespread desire for new ideas about congregational governance, for correcting me when my ideas did not connect with their experience, and especially for laughing at the good bits so that I would be sure to put them in the book. Here are a few of the congregations that have been especially patient with me:

First Unitarian Universalist Church of Annapolis
Congregation Beth Adam, Cincinnati
St. Peter's Lutheran Church, Hilltown, Pennsylvania
Congregational Church of Needham, Massachusetts
Broadway Presbyterian Church, New York
First Unitarian Church of Philadelphia
First Presbyterian Church, Sandusky, Ohio
Unitarian Universalist Church of Greater Lynn, Swampscott, Massachusetts
Centenary United Methodist Church, Winston-Salem, North Carolina

I owe a debt of gratitude to these and many other congregations for allowing me to meddle in their business. Each has picked and chosen from the concepts in this book to shape its own model of governance to fit its mission and traditions; none bears any responsibility for what I say here.

One client that is not a congregation—the Unitarian Universalist Musicians Network—deserves special mention for the imaginative, artful way its leaders worked on its reorganization. Who but a group of musicians would explain a governance restructure using a skit? Under their creative influence, I began to draw the diagrams in chapter 4.

I am grateful to Ann and Fred Stocking, who provided a writer's retreat along the coast of Maine when I especially needed it, and to all who have read and criticized the manuscript and encouraged me to finish it. Special thanks to Alban editor Beth Gaede, who provided her usual close readings and helpful suggestions. Jean Lyles edited the copy further, giving it a high gloss marred only by the errors and odd usages with which I absolutely would not part.

When I began my ministry in 1980, the youngest member of my first church became the church's first music director. As I began to write this book, she and I reconnected after more than twenty years apart and married on December 28, 2006. If parts of this book sound happy, you can thank Susan Land Hotchkiss. Me, too!

This book is dedicated to my colleagues around the Alban Institute consulting table, who have been a rich source of learning and encouragement for me these nine years. No one could ask for a more stimulating group of co-workers, nor could any congregation hope for abler navigators in these chartless and exciting times.

1 :: Organized Religion

Religion transforms people; no one touches holy ground and stays the same. Religious leaders stir the pot by pointing to the contrast between life as it is and life as it should be, and urging us to close the gap. Religious insights provide the handhold that people need to criticize injustice, rise above self-interest, and take risks to achieve healing in a wounded world. Religion at its best is no friend to the status quo.

Organization, on the other hand, conserves. Institutions capture, schematize, and codify persistent patterns of activity. People sometimes say, "Institutions are conservative," and smile as if they had said something clever. But conservation is what institutions do. A well-ordered congregation lays down schedules, puts policies on paper, places people in positions, and generally brings order out of chaos. Organizations can be flexible, creative, and iconoclastic, but only by resisting some of their most basic instincts.

No wonder "organized religion" is so difficult! Congregations create sanctuaries where people can nurture and inspire each other—with results no one can predict. The stability of a religious institution is a necessary precondition to the instability religious transformation brings. The need to balance both sides of this paradox—the transforming power of religion and the stabilizing power of organization—makes leading congregations a unique challenge.

Risks for Congregations

When congregations fail to manage "organized religion" well, they face two special risks. One is the temptation to secure support by pandering to people's fears and prejudices. Finding an enemy to organize against is the easiest and least responsible path of leadership in congregations. The long and bloody history of Christian anti-Semitism, the tragic wars of the Protestant Reformation, and in our own time the deep mutual suspicion among various types of Christians, Jews, and Muslims should alert us that the organizing of religion is a high-stakes game. Preference for one's own group over others is a natural passion that religious zeal can make worse. A primary duty of a congregation is to regulate religious bigotry by teaching the whole scope of its tradition—including the parts about caring for strangers and wayfarers—and by insisting on sound norms of ethical behavior for the congregation and its interactions with the world around it.

The second special risk for leaders is that a congregation can succeed so well at organizing that it loses track of its religious mission. Congregational life becomes so tightly ordered that it squeezes out all inspiration. To historians of religion, the pattern is almost a law of physics: religious energy diminishes from one generation to the next.

Disruptive Influences

Fortunately, inspiration thwarts our best-laid plans. Just when the institutional routine is polished, someone has a new idea. Religious leaders plan worship, education, and social-outreach projects, and define benchmarks, measurable outcomes, and quality assessments. Then somebody says, "Why can't we sing exciting hymns like the new church at the edge of town?" or "We say we teach our children Jewish values. But my kids seem to be learning that Judaism is only for kids." Or, "Thank you, Reverend, for your sermon about Jesus and the rich young man. What do you suppose the Lord would tell our church to do with our endowment?" The more soundly you plan to offer people spiritual insights, the more soundly their insights will disrupt your plans.

Organized religion is a paradox, an oxymoron like "sweet sorrow" or "Hell's Angels." The challenge of organized religion is to find ways to encourage people to encounter God in potentially soul-shaking ways while also helping them to channel spiritual energy in paths that will be healthy for them, the congregation, and the world beyond. Religious leaders who write bylaws would be well advised to do so, as theologian Karl Barth admonished preachers, with the Bible in one hand and a newspaper in the other, holding realism and idealism in a salutary tension.

Need for a Model

In facing this challenge, many clergy and lay leaders have expressed the wish for a clear, up-to-date model of what they should be doing. What clarity they do have generally is patched together from denominational guides, experience in various civic and work settings, and reference books like *Robert's Rules of Order*. All of these have value; none quite fills the bill. Congregations are different from other kinds of organizations; and the world is different from what it was in 1876, when General Roberts wrote, and from the years after World War II when much of the received denominational wisdom about congregations seems to have been set in lead type. Here are some things that seem clear to me as I attempt to meet this need:

There is no one right way to organize a congregation. I do not believe that an original, correct model of leadership can be found in history or Scriptures. History, as I read it, shows that people of faith have chosen a wide range of organizational forms to meet the challenges of their particular times. At any one time, different congregations organize differently because of their different values and the different roles they play in the wider community.

Religious institutions have often borrowed organizational

forms from the society around them: the early Christian churches took on some of the forms of Hellenistic mystery cults, the medieval popes behaved like kings, and the New England Puritans cloned the structure of an English town. Congregations have looked like extended families, noble fiefdoms, parties of reform, cells of resistance, and leagues of mutual protection. Christians often give lip service to the "apostolic church," but few have seriously followed its example of communal property or cheerful martyrdom. Likewise, though Jews love to sing the song "Tradition" from *Fiddler on the Roof,* you could look hard at a Russian shtetl and find little that resembles a Reform temple on Long Island.

I cite this varied history not to be cynical, but to free our thinking from a narrow sense of binding precedent. An awareness of the wide range of forms that congregations of the past borrowed from the world around them frees us to draw wisdom from our own environment. For better or for worse, the main organizational model for contemporary congregations is the corporation, and specifically the nonprofit corporation, which emerged in the late nineteenth century as the all-purpose rubric for benevolent work. For congregations, the nonprofit garb fits pretty well, though not perfectly. What works for other charities may not be so effective or appropriate for congregations. On the other hand, our culture's vast experience with corporate governance offers us a treasure trove of wisdom to draw on. Our challenge is to draw on corporate experience selectively, with a critical awareness of what makes congregations different.[1]

Some mistakes have been made often enough that it is only fair to warn against them. At the very least, some choices have foreseeable consequences. For example, if a board tries to manage day-to-day operations through a network of committees, it will inevitably spend a great deal of its time on operational decision making. This outcome follows simply from the fact that if there is no other place for a buck to stop, it will stop at the board table. Many a board resolves to stop "micromanaging," but until it is willing to delegate real management authority to someone else, the board remains the default chief operating officer.

If this were a "Dummies" book, there would be an icon in the margin every time we came to a cause-and-effect relationship like this. It might show a hand slapping a forehead, or a balloon with "Duh!" However, you are not a dummy, so I trust you will recognize these flashes of the obvious yourself.

We can know good governance when we see it. For all the variety of workable ways to organize a congregation, certain patterns consistently appear when governance goes well. My own list of criteria for measuring the effectiveness of governance in congregations includes the following signs of health:

- A unified structure for making governance decisions. The governing board represents the membership by articulating mission and vision, evaluating programs, and ensuring responsible stewardship of resources. Boards go under various names, including vestry, session, council, trustees, and directors (in this book, I simply call them boards). Boards are usually accountable to the congregation, and sometimes also to a regional or national authority as well. A traditional Quaker meeting acts as its own board, but few other kinds of congregations are willing to require the whole membership to spend the time and energy effective governance requires. Most well-run congregations have a single board with primary responsibility for governance, with clearly defined relationships with other boards, committees, staff, the congregation, and denominational bodies.
- A unified structure for making operational decisions. Program leaders (paid and unpaid) work harmoniously to create effective programs with the support of a structure that delegates authority and requires accountability. Anyone who works successfully in a congregation soon learns that multiple accountabilities are unavoidable. Every staff position has a natural constituency whose wishes sometimes conflict with the expectations of the staff leader or the board. Ef-

fective congregational systems do not eliminate those tensions but give clear guidance about how to manage them. Full-time senior staff members are expected to manage the politics of their positions, while part-time and lower-level staff members have supervisors to do that for them. Above all, delegation and accountability are matched. When a program's goals are set, responsibility is assigned to its leader, and sufficient power[2] is delegated so that it will be fair to hold the leader accountable for the fulfillment of the stated goals.

- A creative, open atmosphere for ministry. Members take advantage of many opportunities to share their talents and interests in an atmosphere of trust and creativity in which structure, goals, and purposes are clear. One of the most helpful findings from research on corporate effectiveness is that the command-and-control approach works for only a narrow range of tasks. Even the military, which highly values obedience, has learned that delegating as many decisions as possible to lower-level people, while giving clear guidance, reduces errors and improves adaptability to changing circumstances. Likewise, no congregation can succeed by relying on its board or staff to come up with all of the ideas. In the most effective congregations, programs and ministries "bubble up" continually from outside the formal leadership.

No list will capture every variation, but where these three criteria are met, I have learned to expect high morale among lay and professional leaders and enthusiastic ownership among the members of the congregation.

Congregations have a lot to learn from other nonprofits, religious and secular. As I have mentioned, nonprofit boards have become more sophisticated. A wide variety of resources have become available to help boards with strategic planning, staff oversight, and policymaking, and with keeping focused on top-level governance—and staying out of management. Few congregations take advantage of these resources. In fact, many religious leaders automatically react against them. "Shouldn't the church be different?" "I didn't become a pastor so I could be a CEO!" "Sometimes at these board meetings I feel as though I were at work!"

Congregations are different from other organizations, but in ways that may not be apparent. The religious mission of a congregation is important but does not distinguish it from other nonprofits founded from religious motives. The most important special features of a congregation have to do with the overlapping of constituencies and the special role of the clergy leader. In a secular nonprofit—say, a mental-health clinic in a poor neighborhood—there is typically little or no overlap between the board, the staff, and the clients. Financial support may come partly from the board but mostly from other government, foundation, and private sources. It would be rare to find that an executive director was counseling someone whose parent was on the board, or that a major donor was also a staff member. In congregations, this kind of role conflict is the rule, not the exception. Many maxims of nonprofit management assume a crisp separation of roles, and treat "role conflicts" as problems to be solved. Congregations need to manage such role conflicts openly and ethically, but they cannot eliminate them without doing violence to the basic nature of the congregation. Nonprofit wisdom needs to be examined and adjusted to fit congregational realities.

Size matters. No single fact tells you more about a congregation than its size, and no statistic better captures the size of a Protestant church than its median worship attendance. For synagogues, the most comparable number is usually the number of member families. Size is as important in the field of governance as in any other aspect of organizational behavior. To sustain itself or to grow (or even to decline gracefully), a congregation's structure needs to be appropriate to the size it wants to be.

The larger a congregation becomes, the more of its behavior is explained by formal documents like bylaws, books of order, job descriptions, and budgets. A small congregation may have all of these documents, but it makes most of its decisions on the basis of an informal pecking order of seniority, relationship, and trust. Who happens to be an officer or board member at the moment means little; and who happens to be pastor means even less.

In a large congregation, formal understandings matter more. These understandings may or may not be in writing. But in large congregations, writing is important; written job descriptions more or less describe real jobs, and governance documents like bylaws actually govern how a congregation operates—at least some of the time. Even in a large church, relationships, longevity, and money still confer informal authority. One minister who has remained in place while his church grew rapidly said, "There are people in this congregation I will have to treat as though we were still small until they die." But as a congregation grows, it cannot leave so much to chance. Leaders do not randomly bump into one another often enough to pass necessary information, establish an informal hierarchy, or smooth over conflicts by the influence of personal friendship. Written policies, role descriptions, procedures, goals, and missions matter a great deal in congregations with more than about 250 active members.

Most of what I have to say in this book will relate to congregations that are at least pastoral-size (with a median attendance of 50 to 150 children and adults). I hope to answer a frequent question from congregations in the pastoral-to-program plateau zone (150 to 250 children and adults): "How do we need to restructure our governance to grow larger?" Congregations stuck at other size transition points (for example, around 400 and 800 in attendance) also need to organize in new ways to break through the barrier. At each larger size, a congregation needs a more clearly articulated structure with an explicitly defined role for each component part. Only by empowering the board, staff, and congregation to play each role to the hilt can a large institution resist the downward pull of habit and rigidity or the centrifugal effect of subgroups digging themselves into private bunkers.

Amid this emphasis on larger congregations, it is important to insert a word about the family-size congregation. About half of North American congregations are family-size, with an attendance of up to fifty children and adults[3], with a "plateau zone" stretching up to one hundred or so. They typically vest tacit governance authority in one or more "matriarchs" or "patriarchs" who may or may not hold official titles. Decision making is informal, and authority belongs to those who earn it through longevity, consistent service, and trustworthy personal relationships. The governing board has authority only when its actions reflect the judgment of the organic leaders. The vision of a family-size congregation is the family's vision as spoken by the matriarchs and patriarchs, and any effort at discernment or strategic thinking needs to happen with and through them. Anyone who tries to practice the fiduciary work of governance—evaluating programs, auditing the books, assuring that the assets are protected—without the blessing of the natural leaders is apt to be met with indignation. In small congregations, leaders rarely think about the congregation as an entity distinct from its members. This attitude is one reason family-size congregations feel refreshingly informal and unbureaucratic, but it creates a risk that leaders may treat tax-exempt assets as personal or joint property. It comes as a surprise to leaders of small congregations when, occasionally, the IRS or the local property assessor takes a nosy interest in family affairs!

Governance and ministry in family-size congregations happen in the same informal way as everything else. Work is done when family leaders assign jobs to people. Susan takes on the annual church fair, John makes sure the lawn is mowed, and Dorothy, who needs help to get out, checks in with people by phone to see that those who need it get the help and support they need. Once assigned, a task often belongs to the same person until he or she dies or locates a successor. Little real authority is delegated with the job; problems, disagreements, and suggested changes go to the matriarchs and patriarchs for resolution. The small congregation makes decisions as a group, and if a lamb strays too far from the flock, there is a shepherd with a crook.

The pastor or rabbi (if there is one) normally plays the role of lamb, not shepherd. Clergy may be treated with respect in a small congregation, but they can lead only within limits set by those who really are in charge. Many denominations place new clergy—fresh from seminary, full of concepts—in small congregations. Eager to take their place as leaders, these new professionals learn that, unless they stay in place long enough to become matriarchs or patriarchs themselves, they must accept a secondary role. One pastor of a small church said, "I imagined myself sitting at the head of the dinner table, but I'm still a guest. They let me say the prayer; then they talk about a life that I'm not part of." Some family-size congregations put new members into board and other titled leadership positions rather quickly—but then, if the newcomers traverse unspoken boundaries, suddenly pull the plug on their apparent power. Change happens in small congregations, but only after consultation and a blessing by the proper elders.

Let this be a caution to readers of this book who serve as clergy in small congregations! Formal structures and small congregations usually do not mix. This is not to say, however, that the underlying concepts do not apply. Governance and ministry are still two different things, even if the same small circle of informal leaders does them both. It can be helpful to separate them, if only into different time slots. Formal titles need to be taken with a grain of salt, but the basic roles of a board still need to be played. It is still helpful to take the right group on a retreat (or into the right living room) to talk about the purpose of the congregation, what it does best, and how it will ensure that property and people are kept safe. The results of such a conversation will travel home from the retreat in the heads of matriarchs and patriarchs, or not at all. The points to keep in mind are that it takes much longer to achieve leadership in a small congregation than in a large one, and that informal leadership matters more than what is said aloud or in writing. Other than that, a small congregation is exactly like a large one!

Ministry and money should not be separated into departments. Many congregation leaders take it for granted that "spiritual leadership" should belong to clergy and "business affairs" to the laity. This dualistic notion has a long history in our culture. Often it comes with a parental attitude by lay leaders who want to protect clergy from contamination by the rough-and-tumble world of power and money. Separating ministry from money teaches by example that pipe dreams of morality do not apply to the world of money, power, and institutions. This arrangement suited Machiavelli, who advised his prince to "learn how not to be good," but it is a sad day when a religious institution parks its spiritual interests in one pigeonhole and its money in another. Dividing faith and money in this way effectively consigns the sovereignty of God to the Hallmark Channel, leaving CNN, the Nature Channel, and FOX Business to the devil.

In congregations, the practical effect is to divide leaders into two groups: the green-eyeshade people serving on the finance, building, and personnel committees; and the rose-colored-glasses crowd that populates the worship, education, and outreach committees. Of course, some people belong to both groups, and it is always possible for capable, well-meaning people to make any structure work harmoniously. As a matter of best practice, though, it is important to remember that no goal is so purely spiritual that it requires no money, space, or time, and that no action is so financial as to lack ethical or spiritual implications. People with differing skills will always differ in their temperaments; visionaries will always, to some degree, come into conflict with bean counters. But there is no need to add force to natural differences by building them into the organizational structure.

Good Advice, Bad Ideas

Traditional "polities," or ways of organizing congregations, typically combine good advice and important values with out-of-date
and flawed ideas. Many Protestant denominations were founded
by people who believed strongly in particular ideas about how to
organize. The names of the main polity families—presbyterian,
episcopal, and congregational—mean, respectively, rule by elders,
bishops, and congregations. One way of looking at such differences is to picture them along a spectrum, with extremely independent polities at one end and tightly connectional ones at the other.

POLITY SPECTRUM

Independent   Connectional

The more connectional denominations issue detailed polity
instructions like the Canons of the Episcopal Church, the United
Methodist *Book of Discipline,* and the Presbyterian *Book of Order.*
But even congregational denominations favor certain organizational practices and discourage others. "Congregational polity"
plays out quite differently depending whether it is practiced by
American Baptists or Southern Baptists, Unitarian Universal-
ists, Disciples of Christ, or the Congregationalists in the United
Church of Christ. Groups of independent congregations declare
their independence in surprisingly connected ways!

A denomination's polity expresses the beliefs of its founders
about who can best discern a congregation's mission and direct its
practice. Today's members may or may not share (or even know
about) the founders' values. Even when they do, the specific institutional practices and structures recommended in the past may

not be the best way to express those values in a changed world, or may not reflect the best wisdom currently available about what works in organizations.

Flaws in Denominational Advice

Almost all denominational advice about governance suffers from two flaws. The first is that it works best in average-size congregations. Usually that means that the advice starts working when worship attendance, including children and adults (or, in most synagogues, the number of member families) reaches about 150, and stops working when it exceeds about 400. Most congregations still fall within this range, but the number of large congregations has grown a great deal since 1900, and the percentage of congregants who belong to them has grown much faster. Larger congregations have long made their own rules, more or less surreptitiously. Now that more congregations are large—or would like to be—we need new, more flexible advice about governance that preserves what is essential in traditional values but works in a larger congregation.

The second common flaw in organizational advice from denominations is that it tends to be problem-centered. This flaw is most obvious when the advice is published in an official manual. At first, such books attempt to set a standard for the normal operation of a healthy congregation. But as years go by, new regulations mainly address problems, conflicts, and scandals. Soon the book contains more pages about problems than about how a healthy congregation can fulfill its mission. It is important to have rules for how to address problems. When congregations and denominations disagree on social or theological issues, for example, it becomes important to know who ultimately owns the property in case of a division. But vital, healthy congregations need advice, too, and often find it hard to come by.

At points throughout this book, I criticize some practices that have become almost sacred in certain denominations. I make no apology for this criticism, nor do I mean to sneer at the denominational staff members who advocate for customary practices. I have been a denominational bureaucrat, and I have been an author, and it is much easier to be an author! Denominational leaders are among the most enthusiastic advocates of fresh approaches, if only because they may see that the old ways are failing before others do. When that happens, they can be great allies to congregational leaders who want help to struggle free from habits of behavior (including but not limited to those promoted by denominations) that prevent them from addressing current needs with vigor and originality.

"Liberal theology" is not the problem, and mimicry is not the answer. Many if not all of the congregations I work with are located to the left of the theological center. By that, I mean they read their scriptures flexibly; they do not claim a monopoly on salvation; and they believe, as the United Church of Christ does, that "God is still speaking." As is well known, the statistical trend for congregations of this type has not been good in recent decades; nonetheless, I reject the view that "liberal theology" is the source of liberal congregations' troubles. In fact, I have a strong hunch that something close to the opposite is true: liberal theology has suffered from poor organizational practices in liberal congregations. It is true that many right-wing churches have enjoyed success because they had outstanding skill at leadership and organization. But well organized congregations are succeeding (and poorly organized ones are failing) across the theological spectrum. The key trait such congregations have in common is their strong belief that they have something vitally important to offer other people. With that conviction, congregations have the courage to let go of old ways of organizing in the hope that new ways might help to achieve their overriding mission. Liberal congregations' problem is not liberal theology; it is their doubt that other people need and want a liberal faith. Lacking this conviction, any congregation clings to familiar structures and resists changes that might help propel its message to a wider public.

I also reject the commonly proposed idea that unsuccessful congregations ought simply to copy modes of governance used by successful ones. Governance in congregations is not the science of achieving optimal results through organizational re-engineering. Governance is an expressive art, like preaching—the forms of our organizations must reflect the values at their heart. Are we called to preach our gospel to those who have not heard it yet? Then we should organize for outreach and evangelism. Do we see the congregation as a little commonwealth, a model for the world to be? Then we are justified in following the enlightened polity we want the world to follow, even if that limits our appeal or means that we make decisions slowly. What will not work is to adopt organizational approaches simply because they work for other congregations or in business or the nonprofit world. We can benefit from the experience of others, but we will not succeed by simply mimicking success.

Congregations can teach civic skills by governing themselves well. I worry that our society is losing necessary skills for group decision making. Electoral politics now happens mostly through mass broadcasts from candidates to individuals in front of television sets or other video devices. We have too few conversations about moral and political issues among people who know and trust each other, but whose economic interests and political philosophies diverge. An increasing fraction of too many people's time is spent at work, often in large organizations that offer little chance to learn the skills of democracy. Young people spend a great deal of time in closely structured programs—for the affluent this means classes, lessons, sports teams, and tutoring designed to optimize their college applications; for the poor it means, increasingly, reform school, prison, and the military. These environments are a poor substitute for programs like religious youth groups, Boy Scouts or Girl Scouts, Junior Achievement, and school governments that at their best were led by youth and adults in partnership. These old ways of building social capital, for all their faults, have not found adequate replacements.

Congregations are among the few remaining settings where people of different ages, occupations, and political philosophies have a chance to mix and be in conversation. The religious roof affords just enough in the way of commonality to make serious conversation possible, but only a few congregations take advantage of this opportunity. No wonder that when congregations can no longer avoid a difficult issue, they so often can respond only by separating the parties. As I write, the most common conflicts in North American Protestant churches are about sexuality and worship style. I see plenty of division and debate about these issues, but too little dialogue. Congregations in our time have an important opportunity for civic education. By daring to keep a few difficult questions on the table at all times and handling the discussion well, a congregation educates its members in the arts and practices of civic life. Society can only benefit.

Art, Not Science

Leaders of communities of faith are never simply managers of institutions, nor do they have the luxury of being purely spiritual leaders. "A purely spiritual religion," James Luther Adams said, "is a purely spurious religion" because it has no power or purchase in the material world.[4] Congregations are vessels of religious growth and transformation—but to be vessels, they need firmness and stability. A congregation easily becomes an end in its own mind—recruiting people to an empty discipleship of committee service, finance, and building maintenance. Institutional maintenance is a necessary, but ultimately secondary, function of a congregation. If souls are not transformed and the world is not healed, the congregation fails no matter what the treasurer reports. Paul of Tarsus put his finger on this tension when he said, "The letter killeth, but the spirit giveth life" (2 Cor. 3:6 KJV).

That is why governance in congregations is not a science but an art. Leaders must continually balance the conserving function of an institution with the expectation of disruptive, change-inducing creativity that comes when individuals peek past the temple veil and catch fresh visions of the Holy.

2 :: Governance and Ministry in Interesting Times

Advice about how to govern faith communities is found in the early literature of most traditions. I am thinking of Paul's letters to the early churches, the teachings of the Buddha for the leaders of sangha communities, the Hadith of the Prophet Muhammed, and the debates of rabbis in the Talmud over the emerging shape of Judaism. All of these writings struggle with the basic paradox of organized religion: how to create a stable institutional environment in which people's lives will be transformed. These texts were written in the wake of soul-shuddering spiritual change. It seems that every transformation of the spirit calls, in turn, for changes in the way communities of faith govern themselves.

Our congregations may or may not face a crisis on the level of the ones just mentioned, but the world in which they work has changed a great deal in the last generation. Meanwhile, many congregations organize essentially the way they did in 1950, with boards and committees dutifully meeting, taking minutes, passing budgets, adopting or defeating motions. Each committee controls all work in its assigned sphere and has to do the work as well. New ideas require many conversations and approvals; old ideas escape serious evaluation. It is a system well designed to resist change, or—to put it differently—preserve tradition.

In the boom days after World War II, resisting change was not so bad. Returning veterans and their families, hungry for stability, flooded into congregations eager to create the stable peacetime world that meant so much to them after the profound disruptions

of the war. Each kind of congregation could count on its defined
market share: Lutherans went to the nearest Lutheran church, Jews
to synagogues, and so on. A congregation's mission was simply to
be the Presbyterian church at Jefferson and Main, or the Reform
temple in Lorain, Ohio. The job of the Lutheran church, then, was
to do as good a job as it could do of being Lutheran. Churches and
synagogues (at least those of certain accepted types) shared a monopoly on the religious interests of a large fraction of Americans.
All they had to do was to be a good example of their type (and
perhaps to move when their constituents did).

Congregations in those days—especially middle-class congregations—had another advantage that has since gone away: an
abundance of skilled labor done for free by women without jobs
outside the home. Top decision-making boards were still mainly
or entirely male, but most of the congregation's work was done by
women. The world of committees, choirs, altar guilds, and children's programs was a woman's world (with, at most, a man at the
head of the table), not to mention women's fellowships and temple sisterhoods, which quietly provided most of the sweat, much
of the money, and a great deal of the spiritual heart. Today, only
in a few wealthy communities is labor from this source obtainable
in such abundance.

It is natural to suppose that the social patterns that prevailed
when we, our parents, or our grandparents were young must have
been in place for centuries. But "housewives" with time to volunteer were a rare, upper-class phenomenon until the prosper-
ous 1920s. During the Depression of the 1930s, almost everyone
was struggling to get by; during World War II, while millions of
men were away, millions of women took factory jobs. The mode
of congregational life that feels "traditional" to most of us today
belongs to 1920–1929 and 1945–1965, periods of general prosper-
ity, domesticity, and (after the war) migration to the suburbs.

The rapid growth of congregations after 1945 sped up a trend
that had begun more than a half-century earlier, toward what some
called the "institutional church." Before 1890, a typical church

building was essentially a room for worship plus a few ancillary rooms (not ordinarily including restrooms). The minister or rabbi worked from his home study, writing sermons and making parish calls on a congregation typically numbering fewer than one hundred active adults. In small towns, clergy often farmed or taught school on the side. Congregations in those days made do with what, to us, looks like a minimum of organizational machinery.

In response to urbanization, industrial development, and the invention of the telephone, that pattern had already begun to change. Around 1890, congregations started to build offices, hire secretaries, install phones, publish newsletters, and canvass for pledges. The minister or rabbi found himself at the head of an increasingly complex institution. Ready or not, congregations coped with budgets, payrolls, fundraising consultants, and a forest of committees and auxiliary organizations. Each of these things existed in a few, mostly urban congregations in the 1800s, but by 1920, many congregations had become true organizations, similar in structure to the corporate charities of the burgeoning "benevolent empire."[1]

Dr. Huffer in Sandusky

One minister who lived uncomfortably through those times of transition was my great-grandfather, Charles Emerson Huffer, who served Presbyterian churches in Indiana, Ohio, Michigan, and Wisconsin during the first decades of the twentieth century. My travels as a congregational consultant sometimes give me chances to visit the towns where Charles Huffer lived and to try to picture what it was like for him to be a minister. I even had the privilege of consulting with the First Presbyterian Church of Sandusky, Ohio, which he served from 1920 to 1925.

With the cooperation of the Rev. Kimberly Ashley and lay archivists, I read seven years of session and trustees' minutes. The 1920s were turbulent years for Presbyterians, marked by anxiety about the loss of Christian influence over the wider culture; worry that churches had gone soft and needed to be made "muscular" again; and conflict over whether Christians should accommodate or rail against new scientific concepts of sexuality, cosmology, and human origins. In these years, Sandusky gradually accepted women's suffrage and the loss of a major employer, the Cleveland and Sandusky Brewing Company, as a result of Prohibition. (H. L. Pecke of Sandusky found a way to link these issues: At a state convention in Columbus, he attacked suffrage as the cause of women's increased drinking![2]) In society as in theology, the 1920s offered more than enough moral grist for any congregation's mill.

Meanwhile, at "Old First" Presbyterian, the trustees discussed the budget, and the session voted people in and out of membership. The congregation met annually to elect, without dissent, slates of elders and trustees. Possibly the church spoke in some way to the great issues of the city or the world during my great-grandfather's ministry, but if so, I find no record of it in the minutes. One thing is certain: in those years, the governing boards—vested, in Presbyterian polity, with great responsibility for spiritual leadership—stuck to a routine of pro-forma votes that today would make the most devoted parliamentarian's eyes bug out with boredom.

One point of mild interest is that toward the end of his Sandusky ministry, Dr. Huffer seems to have gotten into trouble with the board of trustees for failing to raise money energetically enough. In December 1924, the trustees, after voting to pay several bills, including one for $2.01 from Beilstein Laundry, recorded this:

> It was suggested that the Session report the condition of affairs to Dr. Huffer with the view of getting him interested to the extent that he will lend his efforts in raising sufficient money to care for the outstanding indebtedness existing against the church.
>
> There being no further business, the meeting adjourned.

A year and a half later, Charles Huffer had moved on to his next ministry. Apparently, my great-grandfather disappointed the trustees by failing to pay adequate attention to the business aspect of the church. If I needed further evidence for this conclusion, I would find it in a picture of his successor, Dr. Funnell, during whose ministry Old First conducted a successful, professionally run capital campaign, renovated the sanctuary, and increased its operating budget—just in time for the Depression. Dr. Funnell chose to be photographed at his desk, leaning manfully into a black candlestick telephone. "Finally," I can almost hear the trustees sigh, "a truly modern minister."

CHARLES EMERSON HUFFER   ALFRED JENNINGS FUNNELL

Transported to our time, the modern minister of 1925 would find that telephones have changed shape and that they share the office with a multitude of other ways to stay in touch. Women, formerly sequestered in their circles, lead congregations at all levels, lay and ordained. Downtown congregations like First Presbyterian struggle to take hold of a fresh role in ethnically and economically diverse environments. But many governing boards spend time much as they did then: discussing and approving routine matters, authorizing minor spending, and complaining about clergy.

I wonder: why did these men (they were all men, of course) put up with such a gruel-like diet at their meetings? One likely reason is that in those days, an invitation to serve on a Presbyterian session, an Episcopal vestry, or the board of a synagogue was a social honor. One sat at a great table in a room not unlike the library of a good men's club. One followed rituals that would not be out of place in a throne room: hearing reports, acting on petitions, and assenting to the actions of one's ministers. Beneath a formal surface of equality among board members, differences of family, seniority, and wealth created subtle rules of deference that the newcomer was obliged to learn and master or be mortified. The priest, minister, or rabbi held a position of respect and sometimes influence, ranking usually just below the heads of a half-dozen leading families. One knew that the most important work was done outside formal meetings of the board: in committees, private offices, and parlors. Board meetings proceeded with a sense of dignity and order and adjourned at the appointed hour.

If you now serve on a congregation's board, you may have noticed that some things have changed. Most obviously, women have joined most boards; in many, they predominate. Few communities have clear social pecking orders any more, and people who join in group decision making expect to do so as equals. Many members, though, have little or no interest in participating in a congregation's leadership or helping to shape its program. Instead, they join a congregation whose style and leadership feel compatible. If they become dissatisfied, they vote with their feet rather than their hands or voices. Because communities are larger, more religious options are available. People now more often choose to join congregations that are larger—sometimes much larger—than the small-town church many of us take as our unconscious model. And people bring high expectations, asking what a congregation can do for them and also what it will enable and empower them to do for others.

What Makes Governance in Congregations Difficult

Some of what makes governance in congregations difficult is more or less eternal. But our time offers special challenges. I see four trends that seem especially important: the cultural disestablishment of Protestant Christianity; the predominance of paid employment; the growth of a "shopping" attitude; and increasing tensions over clergy, born both of a general distrust of leaders and of the special ambiguities belonging to the pastoral office.

A Disestablished Culture

Many leaders of today's congregations raised their children, or grew up themselves, during the 1950s and early 1960s, when some 70 percent of Americans belonged to congregations and nearly half attended on a given weekend.[3] Choosing and attending a church or synagogue was a powerful social expectation. Sociologist Will Herberg heralded a new, broader religious culture in his 1955 book *Protestant, Catholic, Jew*. By the 1950s, Herberg wrote, Americans' worldview had "lost much of its authentic Christian (or Jewish) content." It did not matter what your religion was; so long as you had one, you were presumed good—as a citizen and as a person. Congregations grew explosively, sales of Bibles boomed while knowledge of the Bible declined sharply, and the distinctive tenets of the various denominations became less important than finding one's social place in the "triple melting pot" of American religious culture.[4] Given the ugly history of religious bigotry and violence and Protestant privilege in the United States, the three-way détente was undoubtedly a forward step. Only a few scholars and religious leaders questioned whether growth in congregations necessarily meant an increase in religious faith.

Today the scene has shifted. Catholic, Protestant, and Jewish are still options for Americans, but the list has grown. Mormons have achieved some level of acceptance, and millions of Americans practice Asian, African, and pre-Christian European faith traditions. Full acceptance of American Muslims has not yet come, though Muslims now outnumber Jews in the United States. Within Christianity, new sects and innovative styles of congregations multiply. The religious landscape of the United States is far more complex and varied than it was in 1955.

For congregations, the increase in religious diversity means that for most Americans, affiliation is a choice, not an obligation. Even in a rural southern town, where to be anything but a churchgoing Protestant is still unthinkable, 150-year-old Baptist, Methodist, Episcopal, and Presbyterian churches on Main Street cannot presume a steady stream of new adherents. On the edge of town, new congregations, often started in abandoned warehouses or stores, compete with long-established churches for the loyalty of old and (most especially) young.

In most of the country, the list of religious choices now includes two fast-growing ones that were almost unknown in 1955: "none of the above" and "spiritual, but not religious."[5] More Americans than ever before believe that you can be a good—or even a devout—person without joining a congregation at all. Just as the established churches had to learn to get along without state sponsorship, congregations now are learning to get along without the widespread notion that nice people go to church (or, as Herberg added, synagogue).

For congregations of the types that were the dominant American religious life-forms of two hundred years ago—Presbyterian, Episcopal, Congregational, Unitarian, and such—this new diversity has been especially hard, because they bear the burden of a privileged past that has not toughened them for today's challenges. Churches and synagogues that had achieved mainstream respectability by 1955 share part of that same challenge, to the extent that they adopted the mentality of privilege of the "mainline" churches.

For Jewish congregations, the clearest sign of the times is the high rate of interfaith marriage. Religiously mixed couples often raise their children as non-Jews (and sometimes as non-anything). Since the central programmatic focus of most synagogues is Jewish education up through bar or bat mitzvah, the attrition of parents who value Jewish education is an existential threat. For many Jewish congregations, the habits of their years of respectability are poorly adapted to a time when, like other Americans, Jews are demanding that congregations make a case for their participation and support.

The Dominance of Paid Employment

A second trend that has crept up on congregations is the growth of work. Since 1950, the productivity of U.S. workers has more than tripled. When productivity grows, a society has three basic options: it can work less, increase taxes, or raise pay. In general, the United States has chosen the third course: we took the cash and worked even more. The consequences are many: we forgo the long vacations, social safety net, and high taxes of most European countries. Instead, working-age Americans spend much more time at work now than a generation ago. The trend toward overwork has accelerated since the middle 1970s, as the richest 1 percent have reaped a growing share of the rewards of increased productivity. Part of the increase in per-capita work comes from the increase in women's participation in the work force. But the hours each worker works has increased too. Add to this the increase in the number of households headed by a single adult, and the result is that a typical working-age family has much less discretionary time to spend volunteering.

The practical effect for congregations is the loss of what had been one of their most critical resources: women willing and able to work for little or no pay. A woman who would once have gladly volunteered to fold the church newsletters every month just to get out of the house, or would have taught Hebrew school to use her college education, now has more than enough chances to do both. On paper, the amount of volunteer time in society has not measurably declined. The number of healthy retired people has increased, and volunteering has become a high priority for many people, thanks in part to schools that require it, congregations that encourage it, and a new breed of nonprofit institutions that market it in new ways. But the pattern of volunteerism has changed, and congregations that recruit volunteers the same way they did in the 1950s feel acutely the loss of younger women's work.

Today's volunteer has higher standards than did volunteers of old. She (or he) requires that the nature and scope of the work be defined honestly and clearly, that the benefits be significant and tangible, and that the work itself make good use of the talents of the volunteer. An institution that, in addition, offers volunteers some personal benefits will out-compete the rest.

The very model of a modern voluntary institution is Habitat for Humanity. Each week, Habitat offers thousands of volunteers finite opportunities for service in which they help create a house that they can see and drive past for the rest of their lives. They can expect to meet the beneficiary—because the family that will live in the house usually works on it with them. They may learn a skill they can use on their own houses. And they become part of a temporary work team in which the likelihood of making friends is high. Congregations that succeed at engaging volunteers follow the example of Habitat, the Girl Scouts, and other well-run modern charities, to the point of rarely using the word "volunteer."

More likely, such congregations will talk about "recruiting people into ministry" or "helping people to identify their gifts." Today's high-expectation volunteers respond when they believe their time will be used well.

Our work-oriented culture affects congregations in another way. People spend so much of their time at work that they learn many of their beliefs and assumptions about organizations from the workplace. If there was ever a time when the domestic sphere had its own mores and values, inculcated in all cultivated people by virtuous women and their friends the reverend clergy, that time has passed. When people think about how congregations should run, their first point of reference in most cases is the way things run at work. The trouble is, they all work in different places and learn different things.

In my first congregation, for example, we were trying to decide whether to move to a new location. Most of the leaders fell into one of three occupational groups. One group, many of them college professors, formed a study committee. It met frequently, gathered information, and debated the implications of the proposed move for our congregation's purpose and identity, without noticeably moving toward a decision. A second group, comprising mostly middle managers from IBM, was comfortable spending quite a bit of money gathering data and expert opinion while deferring any action smacking of commitment. Meanwhile, a retired entrepreneur, acting on his own, plunked down ten thousand dollars of his own money for an option on a piece of land he thought would be perfect for the church. He said, "You have up to a year to make up your minds. If you don't use the option, I will—and I'll resell the land for a profit!" In the end, we bought the land he chose; I am glad we did.

That story ended well despite the lack of insight on all sides. I can't help thinking, though, that we could have made our way more smoothly had we talked about our differing assumptions. Unfortunately, as in many congregations, our culture tacitly discouraged talking about work. In part, this tendency stems from a laudable desire to give every member equal status. What is lost, though, is the chance to take full advantage of the range of gifts among the members.

When the topic under discussion is the governance process itself—how we make decisions, as opposed to what decisions we should make—occupational differences can be quite sharp. Everyone learns important lessons early in life about how to behave in groups, how decisions should be made and justified, and what to do when you do not get your way. In gentler times, those lessons were taught partly at home—and usually in larger families, most of which lived under the guidance of a full-time mother. Today many of us are formed in the artificial "family" of our occupation. Around the board table of a congregation, you can occasionally spot the flabbergasted face of someone learning for the first time that the lessons of his or her workplace are not universally accepted truths.

An interesting sidelight to the theme of occupational differences is that people do not always bring the best of what they learned at work to church or synagogue with them. Sometimes when someone says, "We should do this because it's what we do at work," I ask, "How does it work at work?" and she says, "Terrible!" It is almost as though the congregation were the place to make a bad idea good at last, or to inflict on others what one cannot avoid from nine to five.

The Growth of a "Shopping" Attitude

A third cultural change that makes a difference in what works and doesn't work in congregational governance is that people have new ideas about how to shop for goods and services. In the 1950s, people bought religion pretty much the way they bought *Encyclopaedia Britannica*: the customer paid a sacrificial sum for a lifetime supply of correct answers to all of the most important questions she and her children might ask. Britannica salesmen made house calls and accepted payment in weekly installments. In the early 1990s, this model nearly bankrupted the Britannica Company. Competition from CD-ROM encyclopedias like Microsoft Encarta and the fact that fewer women were at home and willing to receive a salesperson in the daytime were both factors. Still, Britannica might well have continued to sell large numbers of printed encyclopedias if not for an underlying shift in mentality: people no longer believed in the one-source theory of right answers. In its heyday, people paid a hefty sum for *Britannica* because it was *Britannica*. Today, people with questions expect an instantaneous selection of information sources that appear free, courtesy of Google, Yahoo, and their ilk.

Similarly, visitors to worship once shopped (if they shopped at all) for a single source for their religious answers, spiritual home, and social identity. Today, shoppers look for the best buy and are always prepared to change brands, even when the "vendor" is a congregation. Some prefer an undemanding congregation that delivers standard product at low cost, like Wal-Mart. Others look for something more along the lines of Levenger's eighteen-hundred-dollar desk—an affirmation of the buyer's taste, judgment, and discretionary wealth. The few who choose a strenuous religious life will look for congregations offering a religious discipline analogous to hiking gear from REI.

Certain congregations, all across the spectrum and across denominational lines, have learned to thrive in this competitive environment. Even Britannica eventually recovered from its doldrums. It released, in time for Christmas 1997, a CD-ROM edition with abundant links to information on the Web. For about one hundred dollars plus updates, the consumer got Britannica's help sorting information wheat from information chaff. Today Britannica offers the same service on the Web.[6]

A few major players like the Southern Baptists, Mormons, or Roman Catholics may thrive—as Starbucks and Google do—because of the perceived uniqueness of their brand. But for most congregations, the old single-source model does not work, because people today believe it is better to shop than to be loyal to a brand.

Leaders tempted to complain about "church-shoppers" might consider this point: churches shop, too. So do synagogues. Once upon a time, most congregations procured most or all of their curriculum materials, worship helps, and outside speakers from one source: the denomination. They relied on regional and national offices to train and supply clergy, organize their missionary work, advise them about governance, and consult with them in times of conflict.

For these services, congregations transferred a high percentage of their local revenues to national denominational and missionary bodies. One of the most striking trends in congregational finance is the decreasing proportion of local revenues that transfer in this way.[7] Congregations prefer to choose their curricula, worship materials, and social ministries themselves. Even clergy, especially those in junior roles, are chosen in a wider-than-denominational marketplace. In short, congregations should not be surprised that people shop: they do it, too.

Tension over Clergy

The fourth and last "new" factor I will mention, tension over clergy, is anything but new. One of the first recorded church fights, the Donatist controversy of the fourth and fifth centuries, was about whether you could go to heaven by receiving sacraments from a priest who led an immoral life or who held heretical beliefs. At that time, with assorted christianities in circulation and a variety of notions about how priests should behave, a lot of priests had to be wrong one way or another. Did that mean the souls under their care were damned? It was a reasonable question. The church as a whole rejected Donatism, but it has never rid itself entirely of the idea that clergy need to match, in holiness, the One they represent on earth.

Add to that the expectation that the clergy should equal executives in business skills, psychologists in counseling, and TV anchors in mellifluousness, and you can see why congregations often find their clergy falling short. A built-in tension between clergy and laypeople has existed whenever and wherever congregations have attempted to include both. Governing documents frequently express ambivalence about how much power to grant clergy, either treating them as sovereign in their sphere or hemming them in as though hierarchy (literally, "rule by priests") were the greatest risk a congregation had to face. At the root of the ambivalence, I think, is the persistent concept that the priest's, minister's, or rabbi's job is to resemble God. On the one hand, that expectation sets impossible performance standards; on the other, it makes some people overreact to clergy leadership, because they confuse the power of a clergy leader with the power of God.

Not everyone is so reactive. Mature and older leaders, who have seen clergy come and go before, can often damp down congregational reactiveness. Such leaders have an opportunity to foster spiritual maturity in others. After all, what could be more important than to learn that finite representatives of God—the clergy or the congregation—are not God? We all know this in our heads, but as life disappoints us and our losses multiply, we have to learn it again and again.

Clergy earn a lot of the criticism they receive. But you only have to be there when one announces his or her resignation to see how inappropriately strong some people's reaction is. Quite simply, people confuse the messenger with the message. If a clergyperson's job is to reflect and exemplify the steadfast love of God, how should congregants take it when theirs says, "I have decided there is something I would rather do than be your minister"? From a human being, such an announcement is understandable; from God's emissary, it can feel like a calamity.

Clergy, and especially clergy who serve congregations, live the paradox of "organized religion" intimately, day after day. Cogregations invite people to bring their highest, most religious expectations with them when they come; we can hardly be surprised when the best we can offer sometimes comes as a disappointment. The person who is most apt to disappoint people is the clergy leader. One big difference between the role of clergy in congregations and CEOs, curators, presidents, and executive directors is the intensity with which people vest them with responsibility for the success not just of the institution but also of their own religious quests.

The combined force of these environmental changes—disestablishment of churches, the predominance of work, the rise of "shopping" as a frame for the religious journey, and increased reactiveness toward clergy—makes this a good time for congregations to consider fresh ways of organizing that will help them to meet fresh challenges.

3 :: How Congregations Organize

American religious life, for all of its diversity, has a strong conformist strain. Congregations from a wide range of traditions organize according to a few common templates. The differences between church "polities" (congregational, episcopal, and presbyterian)—not to mention the diversity of global cultures represented in American religion—do make a difference, especially when it comes to choosing clergy or addressing conflict. But even congregations with strong ethnic and sectarian roots eventually absorb the organizational forms they see around them: paid clergy, elected boards, congregational meetings, and committees. With the forms come certain implied assumptions—for example, that the congregation's purpose is to meet its members' needs; that it should run itself without much meddling from denominational officials; that clergy should defer to laity; and that laity speak their most authoritative word by voting. The resulting way of organizing, which sociologist Stephen Warner calls "*de facto* congregationalism,"[1] helps make American religion democratic, lively, fractious, adaptable, and accessible. It also drains great tempests of ecclesiastical variety into a few well-worn organizational ruts.

As a consultant, I have worked with hundreds of congregations from well over a dozen faith groups in the United States and Canada and have found them fascinatingly diverse in some ways and numbingly alike in others. Even where a central hierarchy controls important aspects of a congregation's life (as in United Methodist, Christian Science, or Presbyterian congregations), whatever is left to be controlled internally tends to be handled in one of a few ways. I see three broad patterns commonly in use.

The Board-centered Congregation

Congregations usually start with a cadre of highly energetic and committed members. When the group grows to the point of wanting anything so formal as a board, it naturally calls on those who have taken charge of pieces of its practical work: music, education, building, finance, publicity, membership, and so on. The resulting structure, which often persists even when the congregation is much larger, is shown in figure 3.1

Figure 3.1

BOARD-CENTERED

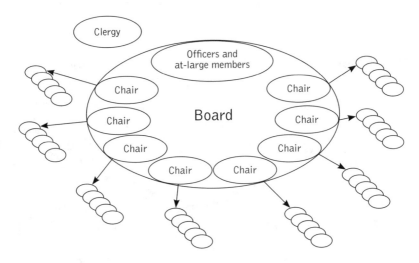

Most board seats are filled by leaders of program and administrative areas, who are generally called committee chairs, though an actual committee may or may not exist. A few board seats are filled—depending on the polity—by a lay or clergy chairperson, secretary, and treasurer, plus one or more "at-large" members of the board.

For small congregations, this is a good, workable board structure. With all of the important leaders in the room, questions large and small can be answered on the spot. Board members have earned leadership status by taking responsibility. As leaders of the congregation's daily work, they use board meetings to coordinate activities, work out differences, and give each other information, counsel, and support. The board agenda often consists mainly of a round-robin of reports, with the board stopping to discuss anything in a report that interests the members and taking action as required to authorize spending, resolve differences, or improve on a committee's work. Everybody gets to hear what's happening in everybody else's area. There is little need to publicize the board's decisions, because almost everyone who needs to know is already at the meeting or works closely with somebody who is. In small congregations, people find it difficult to see how else a board might be assembled, or what else it might do.

The board-centered structure works fine so long as the congregation stays small. But if it grows, programs multiply, and so do the disadvantages of the board-centered structure. Adhering to the theory that important programs deserve board representation, the board gets larger and board meetings longer. Each board member spends most of the meeting hearing about areas of interest and responsibility other than his or her own. For committee chairs, the monthly board meeting is just the beginning: each has (at least in theory) a committee meeting to attend, and on top of that an actual program to run. That's three jobs—no wonder it so often becomes difficult to recruit board members! Especially when incumbents wail a righteous noise about their burdens, as too many do, others understandably avoid signing on for a job that requires so many evenings away from home.

The board-centered structure has the virtue of stability. Lyle Schaller used to call family-size congregations "cats"—nobody owns them, and they have nine lives. Denominational officials often want to close them down to start a larger congregation in the same location, but you can't kill them with a stick. The board-centered structure is one of the small-congregation bulwarks against change. Standing committees, by their nature, resist new ideas, because new ideas require new work and new expenses. Standing committees already have plenty of work piled on their plates and plenty of ideas for their finite budgets. Standing committees resist change naturally; a board made up of chairs of standing committees resists change reflexively.

A board made up of practical program leaders has trouble talking about anything but practical program issues. In a small congregation, the board focuses on program administration because there is no one else to do it. Other functions of a board, like discernment, goal setting, and evaluation, happen, if they happen at all, at an annual retreat. An outside facilitator and a change of venue help to shift the mood. Most of the time, though, a board made up of managers will manage—it can't help it. The larger the congregation, the less satisfactory this structure is, and the more the congregation needs a board that rises above day-to-day concerns to think about the bigger picture, not just annually but all the time.

In congregations, each program or administrative area is also a special-interest group. There's nothing wrong with that: we expect musicians to campaign for music, finance people for financial prudence, social activists for social action, and so on. But the board's responsibility is to the mission of the congregation as a whole, so a board member who is there to "represent" a committee must overcome at least a mild conflict of interest.

An example from outside the world of congregations may help illustrate some of these points. Since 1905, most of the fifty board

members of the American Red Cross have been of two types: a
small number of presidential appointees (some of whom were
too important to attend meetings) and representatives of the state
chapters. The chapters were integral parts of the Red Cross, not
separately incorporated. Still, chapters functioned semi-autono-
mously, and "their" board members vied actively to maximize the
share of national resources available to their respective chapters.
At worst, board meetings looked like logrolling sessions in the U.S.
Congress, with the pursuit of common mission overwhelmed by
competition to divide the spoils. In the aftermath of serious financial problems in the national body, regulators naturally asked,
"Where was the board?" Later on, an independent study of Red
Cross governance concluded that the board had several problems,
one of which was that the "representatives" found it difficult to
transcend separate chapter interests well enough to pursue the
common mission or to watch the common till.[2]

You can see the same phenomenon on a less dramatic scale
at budget time in many congregations. A board member selected
from (or by) a program group like education, music, or social justice will tend to advocate for the interests of that program area,
negotiating or contending for advantage. There is no harm in this
advocacy, except that it bypasses the "interest" of the board itself,
which is to look after the mission of the congregation as a whole.
At worst, instead of formulating a common vision of ministry
that would attract greater support, the board becomes a venue
for competing parts of the community to vie for a bigger slice of
a shrinking pie.

If there is a clergy leader, the board-centered structure tends
to leave his or her position more or less ambiguous. In a family-
size congregation, this ambiguity is an accurate reflection of the
truth. But as the congregation grows, the one full-time staff member tends to take de facto charge of many things, simply because
he or she is on the scene. Unless the board takes steps to delegate

authority more clearly to the clergy leader, the gap between the actual scope of his or her authority and what has actually been authorized can become rather large.

The Committee-centered Congregation

The second class of governance structures, and the most common, is the one I call "committee-centered." The committee-centered model is so common that many people assume that it is the only proper way to run a church or synagogue. An observer from Mars might be forgiven for supposing that the chief religious rite of Earth religion, at least in North America, is the committee meeting.

Figure 3.2

THE BOARD EVOLVES...

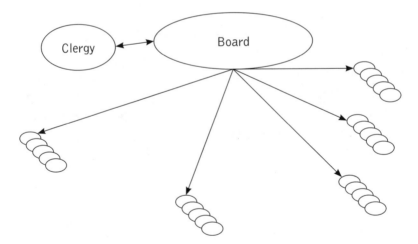

The essential trait of the committee-centered model is that both governance (deciding "what" and making sure it happens) and ministry (deciding "how" and doing it) are delegated by the board to its committees. Or perhaps "granted" is a better word than "delegated," because authority, once granted, tends to reside with the committee, not the board. Committee-centered congregations often adhere to the Map Theory of Committees, in which every inch of programmatic territory belongs to a standing committee, as though the congregation's ministry were a country needing to be split up into states, with no frontiers or unincorporated territories open to homesteaders. According to the Map Theory, if an idea involves music, it has to go before the music committee, and so on. The Map Theory creates a bias against change by putting standing committees in a position to veto change—which, because they have their hands full, they are naturally inclined to do.

The committee-centered structure has arisen, in part, as a solution to the problems of board-centered governance, which increase as congregations grow. Instead of shifting decisively away from the board-centered structure to something else, boards make small adjustments. Committee "liaisons" may replace committee chairs as members of the board. But the board continues to think of itself mainly as a clearinghouse for issues that arise in the course of the real work, which happens in committees. Gradually the action, and the real power, does shift from the board to the committees.

Figure 3.3

SUPER COMMITTEES EMERGE...

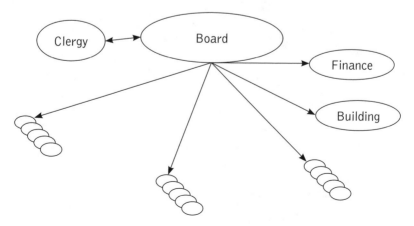

Instead of setting overall direction, the board spends most of its time responding to requests—for money, for permission, for approval, for comment—from the committees. The board becomes a sort of appellate court, deciding questions from people who do not like the answers they get elsewhere in the organization. Over time, the board cedes much of its power to initiate action and becomes reactive, giving and withholding its assent to requests brought to it by others. Sometimes board members actually object to the board's taking any action that has not been thoroughly pre-processed by one or more committees.

All committees are equal, but as committees become more numerous, some of them—"supercommittees" like finance and property—become more equal than others, because they control resources the other committees need. Each committee finds itself in a triangular relationship—reporting to the board but also needing to petition the supercommittees for resources. As family therapists are fond of pointing out, triangular relationships tend to create opportunities for problems. Triangles build anxiety, especially when boundaries and responsibilities are not clearly defined.

Figure 3.4
TRIANGLES BEGIN TO FORM...

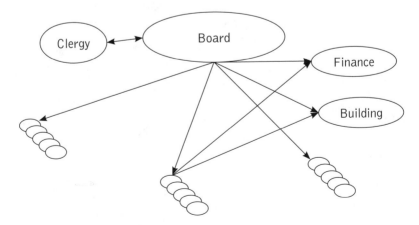

As a glance at figure 3.4 will show, a multitude of triangles appear in the committee-centered structure, especially in larger congregations. The board may or may not have clarified its working relationship with the main clergy leader, but with the hiring of an additional staff member, things get complicated. Every staff member in a congregation has a natural relationship with a particular constituency and its committee. At the same time, he or she has a relationship with the clergy head of staff and with the board. Triangular relationships run a special risk known to systems theorists and family therapists. If each of these relationships is not carefully defined so that it is clear which issues belong to which relationship, then triangles become "triangulation," and anxiety begins to build throughout the system.

Figure 3.5

A STAFF MEMBER IS ADDED...

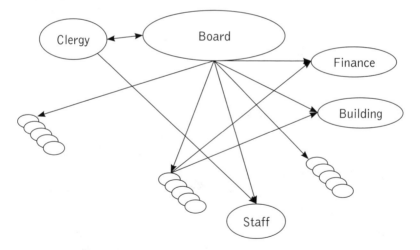

One of the most frequent ways committee-centered congregations fall into conflict is that committees triangulate "their" staff member into advocating change. A ritual committee, for example, might goad an assistant rabbi into championing Jewish contemporary worship. Another staff member (perhaps the cantor or the senior rabbi) reacts by taking the role of "conservative," and the two of them duke it out. One of them may even have to leave—all without direct, open conversation among congregants about their worship style. Because of triangulation, the right people never talk to one another directly.

Figure 3.6
ADDITIONAL STAFF...

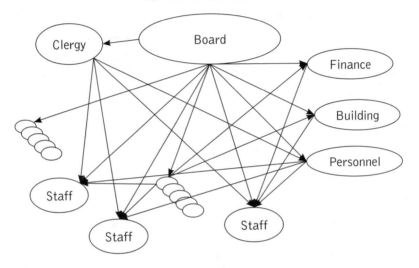

With the addition of a second or third program staff member, a new supercommittee emerges. I will call it "personnel," though it may have another name like "mutual ministry," "staff-parish," or "ministerial relations." This committee often tries to play the roles normally played by a supervisor: setting goals, evaluating, and adjusting individual salaries. When a personnel committee invites church members to express criticisms of staff members to the committee rather than directly, it practices the most troublesome kind of triangulation. Anyone who tries to "fix" the relationship of two others is likely to fail and certain to increase anxiety, especially for himself. Personnel committee members often hear complaints from their friends about a staff member they helped choose—already that's a triangle. A committee member who goes to the staff member to relay what "I've been hearing people say" creates more triangles; congregants who take complaints about staff members to the personnel committee open up yet more, and when complaints go from there anonymously to the head of staff or board, the world begins to fill with anxious triangles. Everyone is helped to feel at least a little guilty, but no one is empowered to address the problem or to say definitively that the problem will remain unsolved.

Figure 3.7
COMMITTEE-CENTERED

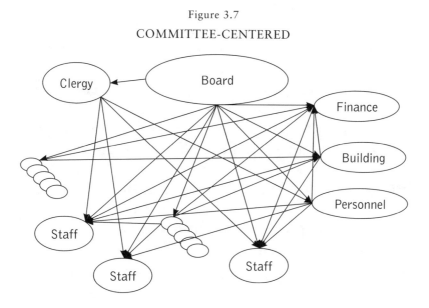

When the personnel committee's role with the staff team is not clearly defined vis-à-vis the head of staff, especially problematic triangles result. In many congregations, the personnel committee hangs out its shingle as a problem solver, mediator, or ombudsperson for the staff—in effect, an alternative boss for anyone who does not like the real boss. Triangles multiply. Figure 3.7 shows a full-blown case of the committee-centered structure.

Skilled leaders can make virtually any structure function flexibly and well. But the committee-centered structure does not make innovation easy. What it does best is what it was designed to do: prepare the congregation and its program for next year, provided that next year is 1959. Here are some common, less helpful features of the committee-centered model:

1. A passive board that spends most of its time listening to reports, responding to proposals, and arbitrating conflicts rather than envisioning the future, creating long-term goals and policies, and ensuring organizational performance. A committee-centered board has little or no agenda of its own—only the sum of the agendas of its committees. Ironically, this way of spending the board's time often means that the board hardly ever talks about the topics it agrees are most important. As a test of a board's committee-centeredness, try this: Ask board members to list the two or three most important things the congregation does: they may say holding public worship, reforming the city, producing educated Jews, or transforming hearts and lives in Jesus Christ. Then ask when they last had a board conversation about trends in worship music, how the city will look when it is reformed, how educated Jews differ from uneducated ones, or how you can tell that a soul has been transformed. A committee-centered board rarely talks about such concerns except, perhaps, when an outside facilitator prompts members to discuss them at a retreat. Instead, it talks about issues that arise out of the congregation's mission; for example, whether to change building locks or to add a staff position—all issues that may be connected in some way to the core mission, but that do not help the board address the heart, the core, the why of it. That is the committees' job!

2. A miserly approach to delegation, in which boards and committees approve projects provisionally and then bring them back repeatedly for criticism, reconsideration, and approval of next steps. This process is frustrating, especially to people who are used to leading major projects, from start to finish, in their work lives. Unfortunately, it can be attractive to people—volunteers and staff alike—who prefer not to be held accountable. In a system that gives no one full authority to carry out a project, there are always plenty of excuses for the absence of results.

3. A fragmented staff whose members connect more strongly with their natural constituencies—educators with parents, musicians with the choir, administrators with the finance committee— than to the staff as a team. Faced with a threatening multiplicity of triangles, many staff members will lay claim to a piece of turf and wall it in. Too often, the result is a collection of disconnected fiefdoms with no accountability for overall results, and a strong tendency for staff members to fall into conflict with anyone who trespasses against them.

The net result of all these features is a congregation that strongly resists change. Imagine that you're a newcomer to a congregation, and you have a new idea. Suppose your idea is significant enough that it requires money, staff time, and building space to succeed. How many places can you go, in the committee-centered structure, if you want someone to tell you no? Lots of places! You can be rejected by the committee that controls the territory on the map where your idea falls. If that's not enough, the finance, personnel, and building-and-grounds committees all will have good reasons not to try it. Or you might go to the clergy head of staff, who knows how things are done—and therefore knows why your idea can't be done. You can even go to the board, which will, after discussion, refer you to a suitable committee, on the grounds that nothing should be voted on unless it is approved by the appropriate committees. Most people never try to run this gantlet; successful innovators often bypass it entirely.

Why do we use committees as the all-purpose instrument of governance and ministry? Perhaps it's in our national blood. The Continental Congress, our first effort at national governance, operated like a committee-centered congregation. David McCullough reports that most of the committees were "chosen with little or no reference to their expertise or abilities, which meant they were usually incapable of getting much done.... General Washington often complained of being bombarded with queries from so many different committees that he wondered if he would have time to fight the war."[3]

From the beginning, the committee has been part of our idea of democracy, used for much too wide a range of purposes. We call people together to make decisions, to gather and reflect on information, to socialize, to serve others, to do work, and to be fed spiritually. But our organizational imagination is so limited that we use one format—the committee—for all these purposes and more. Luckily, not every congregation follows the committee-centered model fully, and most that do have talented leaders who can achieve results even when the system makes that difficult. The committee-centered system, invented for the requirements of a very different world, is urgently in need of change, and many congregational leaders understand this need.

The Staff-centered Congregation

The shortcomings of board- and committee-centered governance have not gone unremarked. On the contrary, at least since the late 1960s, an attack on hidebound, plodding, bureaucratic churches and synagogues has been a frequent theme for advocates of congregational reform. The alternative that has received the most attention sometimes goes under the names "permission-giving" or "purpose-driven."[4] To focus on the organizational aspects, I call this family of governance models "staff-centered."

Figure 3.8
STAFF-CENTERED

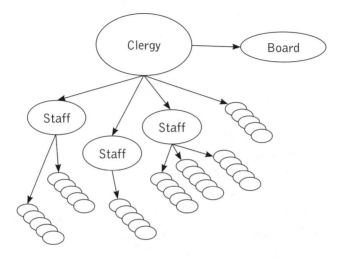

The staff-centered model starts with a charismatic clergy leader who articulates the congregation's mission and vision and recruits "ministry teams" of paid and unpaid staff to carry it out. The vision is so clear that someone with a new ministry idea can usually perceive immediately whether it fits or not. In contrast to the committee-driven congregation, it is easy in the staff-centered model to find someone who can say yes to a new idea: a staff member or the pastor is empowered and encouraged to say yes, giving permission for an unlimited variety of "ministries," all under the umbrella of a central, driving purpose.

Where the staff-centered model is followed consistently, the pastor's role is visionary and entrepreneurial. The staff-centered congregation aims for a minimum of organizational busywork and a maximum of opportunities for anyone who wants to get involved in ministry. The "purpose-driven" and "permission-giving" visions feed a hunger among congregational leaders who find the old ways lacking. Many leaders long to streamline structures, so that deliberative processes do not get in the way of ministry.

One congregation that chose to head in this direction coined a slogan to describe its governance reforms: "Fewer meetings, more ministry!" Some of the largest, most successful congregations in the country operate this way. What's not to like?

The staff-centered model, like the others, does have some built-in disadvantages. One is a certain brittleness and vulnerability resulting from its strong dependence on one leader. If that leader leaves or dies or is discredited, the institution can take a long time to recover. This problem can be mitigated by preparing a succession plan, either among the staff or through the board (yes, even a permission-giving church has a board!). But depending heavily on a sole leader creates a fragile institution, and this drawback cannot be avoided altogether.

A second disadvantage of staff-centered structures is a disadvantage only if you believe, as I do, that committed groups are capable of making better decisions than individuals can. I don't always enjoy group decision making, but I have found again and again that a community willing to be patient with people's differences and indecision will correct and improve the insights of even the most gifted individuals. If you agree with me that wide participation adds an essential element to a congregation's search for truth, then a strictly staff-centered congregation seems wrong. Even if the staff-centered model were always more effective at producing practical results, it would leave me dissatisfied, because it does not make use of every member's gifts for discerning the congregation's mission. This concern, at bottom, is theological: I think each of us comes with a built-in antenna tuned to the right frequency to hear the promptings of the Spirit, and that congregations ought to take advantage of it. I also believe that what people call the "politics" of congregations has a good side, because a group in holy conversation can perceive more about what is good and right than the sum of what its members can perceive alone. People who agree with me, or who believe something similar, choose congregational participation with its messiness, even as we some-times envy the efficiency of the staff-centered way.

What I want, actually, is both. Occasionally I see a congrega-tion that manages to balance the efficiency and clarity of the staff-centered model with other values like democracy, participative decision making, and group discernment. In the next chapter, I will describe how I think this balance can be struck.

Some Even Worse Ideas

First, though, I need to mention several even worse ideas I have run across in my consulting work. Usually the people who prac-tice them do so under the impression that denominational polity requires them, or that they are widespread. The fact that one or both of these impressions may be correct does not make the ideas any better.

Elected Committees and Committee Chairs

In some congregations, mostly in New England, the congrega-tional meeting elects every committee chair and sometimes every committee member as well. It is hard to imagine a less meaningful exercise of democracy than to vote on a slate of between thirty and 120 nominees. Who is empowered by this system? It might seem to be the nominating committee, but in practice, what happens most of the time is that the de facto leader of each committee (who may be a staff member) ends up doing most of the recruiting, and the official nomination process is as empty as the election.

Staff Reporting to Committees

When board- and committee-centered congregations engage paid staff, they sometimes struggle to find language to describe how staff members should relate to one another and to the rest of the organization. Especially if the staff person leads a program area like education, music, or youth work, "owned" by a committee, it seems natural that the committee should hire, orient, and supervise the new staff person.

Dial the clock forward ten years. The staff member is full-time, still working "for" a committee (though by then he or she may actually handpick its members), and in conflict with another member of the staff, possibly the senior clergy leader. What is the process then? Do you assemble the two staff members and their respective committees to try to reach a solution? Do you all go to your mutual boss, the board, and ask it to judge the case? If the congregation elects both the committee and the board, does the congregation have to vote?

Having seen all of these methods tried, I have concluded that "a staff member reports to a committee" is one of those things that you can say in English but that makes no sense, like "rite of caster fish." Committees simply cannot supervise paid staff, because they are not present when the work is done, and it is too difficult for them to speak with one voice. A staff member deserves a boss who works at least as many hours a week as he or she does. Others can participate in the evaluation process or in making policies about staff treatment. But a congregation that wants to remain sane will set its staff up as a single team and hold it responsible for sustaining its own working relationships. Designating someone to be "head of staff" or "leader of the staff team," and requiring the staff team to make its own plans, resolve its own conflicts, and carry out its own evaluations—inviting others to participate in all of these except the conflicts—gives the staff the space it needs to operate effectively.

Multiple Governing Boards

Some congregations have two, or even three, top boards, all responsible directly to the congregation. Sometimes the division reflects an old-fashioned mom-and-pop dualism: the trustees

(Dad) control the money, while a program board (Mom) does most of the work. Sometimes one board is said to be responsible for the "business" aspect of the congregation, while the other takes charge of the "spiritual" part. Have I made it clear yet that I don't like this way of splitting up the universe? Whoever controls "business" ends up having ultimate control of spiritual matters also.

A congregation can create as many boards as it wants, though legally the state will recognize only one of them as "the board" of the corporation. When two (or sometimes even three or four) boards stand together at the top of the organization chart, it is apt to be unclear which buck stops where. In practice, multi-board arrangements tend to act out to excess the dualism their designers had in mind: Trustees manage the money without thinking about the mission, and the "program" board does just the opposite. When everyone gets along, communicates well, and pays attention to the whole, the worst consequence is a strong bias against anything new. At other times, the system can become a setup for the boards to fall into conflict based on the differences between the value systems into which they have been cast.

It does make sense to have a separate board for a substantial subsidiary enterprise, such as a housing project or a nursery school, which requires more expertise and attention than the church governing board can give.[5] A congregation with a large endowment fund may want a separate board (or even a separate corporate entity) to counterbalance the temptation for the governing board to dip into the endowment principal to solve short-term financial problems. In general, though, it makes sense to put one board clearly at the top of the heap, responsible to the congregation for the performance of all others. If more than one board reports to the congregation, the congregation itself must be prepared to resolve differences between them. It is a rare congregation that is disciplined enough to oversee one board adequately, let alone two or three.

Jumbo Boards

Congregations that grow sometimes expand their board proportionately—basing that action, I suppose, on a vague theory of proportional representation. Such expansion would make perfect sense if a board member's job were to represent a certain number of constituents. But if a board's job is to make sure the congregation adheres to its mission and purpose, it is important that it be the right size for that task. Boards with more than twelve or thirteen members find it difficult to think imaginatively as a group or to stay focused on a finite set of board priorities. Large boards, as a rule, tend to be more passive and less able to engage the staff as strong partners. Attendance becomes less consistent, a tendency that makes it difficult for the board to sustain a train of thought from month to month. In effect, the board becomes a miniature congregational meeting.

For a board to act as a board—that is, to envision the future, engage in strategic thought, and hold its own members and others accountable for organizational performance and stewardship—the ideal size is about six to eight, and certainly no more than twelve.

"Suspending the Bylaws"

Sometimes, in frustration with the problems of the governance structure they have, congregations will do something called "suspending the bylaws." I am not sure where this idea comes from—maybe it is an extension of "suspending the rules," which is a bit of *Robert's Rules* arcana meaning to do something slightly outside normal procedure. Suspending the bylaws is more like suspending the Constitution: if it ever happens, I hope to have some bottled water in the basement. A congregation that suspends or repeals its bylaws is governed instead by the state nonprofit corporation statute, which may have some quite specific provisions you do not want to know about.[6] In chapter 8, I will describe a less drastic approach to trying an experiment with governance. In the meantime, if someone proposes suspending the bylaws, suggest cooling off and thinking of something safer.

On to Some Better Ideas

Having wandered for a season in the wilderness of bad ideas, we can now move on to work on something better. The simplicity of the board-centered structure is fine for small congregations that intend to stay small—in other words, for about half of North American Protestant churches, and many urban synagogues and rural Orthodox and Catholic parishes. Congregations that do grow much beyond an average attendance of about 150 seem to go in one of two directions: One is the committee-centered structure, with its highly change-resistant system of triangulated fiefdoms. The other is the staff-centered model, which depends heavily on one strong leader who engages everybody else in ministry, but keeps members at the periphery of the process of discerning and articulating mission.

Sadly, in many mainstream congregations, here is where the conversation about governance reaches a full stop. It is a comment on the limits of our cultural imagination that we so often see the empowerment of leaders and the empowerment of followers as a strict trade-off, a game with a zero sum. A few congregations, though, have pioneered modes of governance that honor congregational participation while charging ministry leaders to use and to share "permission" freely. For me, a good summary of the requirements of good governance in congregations could be phrased as a question: "Can a democratic congregation and an effective governing board operate in partnership with a strong, permission-giving ministry-team structure?" Some of the most vibrant congregations, across the spectrum theologically, are answering this question "Yes!"

4 :: A Map for Thinking about Congregations

Analogies are useful but tricky. New Testament writers compare the church to a human body, a herd of sheep, a bride, and a vineyard. Synagogues are often likened to a house, a tent, or an extended family. None of these comparisons is meant to be exact or literal; a church may act in some ways like a herd of sheep, but a wise leader doesn't plan for that. Poets do exaggerate sometimes!

In the same spirit of poetic license, it may at times be useful to compare the clergy leader of a congregation to a corporate CEO, its members to customers or stockholders, or its staff to the employees of a charity. We can draw many useful analogies between congregations, other nonprofits, and businesses, but ultimately congregations need language and ideas of their own. It is easy to say that "the church should run more like a business" without recognizing that in some respects, churches should and do run very differently. In talking about governance in congregations, we can't completely avoid borrowing language and ideas from other kinds of organizations, but it's also important to use words and images that remind us we are talking about something special.

Collaborative Leadership

Most leaders can see what they don't like about their current structure. It is not so easy to envision how that structure might improve or how it would work afterward. My intention in this book is not to prescribe a specific model of congregational governance but to offer a framework within which congregations can make choices. Those choices will and ought to vary, because how a congregation makes and carries out decisions is a primary expression of its values.

On the other hand, when people complain about their congregation's current structure or imagine how they would like it to change, some themes come up again and again. When I work with leaders interested in governance reform, I often ask them to describe the virtues they would like their new structure to have. "What would you like life to be like for the governing board? How about for the leaders of your programs? What difference would a good structure make for ordinary members of the congregation?" To be effective in governance and ministry, a congregation needs:

- *A unified structure for making governance decisions.* The governing board represents the membership by articulating mission and vision, evaluating programs, and ensuring responsible stewardship of resources.
- *A unified structure for making ministry decisions.* Program leaders (paid and unpaid) work harmoniously to create effective programs with the support of a structure that delegates authority and requires accountability.
- *A firm and well-marked boundary,* with active mutual communication and accountability, between governance and ministry.

Together, these criteria create a standard against which any proposed governance reform can be measured. When met, they tend to foster a creative, open style of ministry, in which members can take advantage of many opportunities to share their talents and interests in an atmosphere of trust and creativity, and in which structure, goals, and purposes are clear. Congregations will assign different weights to underlying values like democracy, efficiency, and freedom. But a wide range of congregations have found it helpful to measure the results of their reflection against these three touchstones.

Governance and Ministry

In the three criteria, I use the words *governance* and *ministry* to differentiate two spheres of leadership in congregations. We could use other words: governance is sometimes called board work, trusteeship, policymaking, or oversight. Instead of ministry, we could say executive or program leadership, staff work, or administration. Other words might fit better in a particular tradition—and I would encourage you, if other words fit better in your setting, to go ahead and use them. I use governance and ministry because they seem to work reasonably well in a variety of congregations. We will define both of these terms more formally later; for now, it is enough to say that governance includes the top-level tasks of articulating the mission, selecting a strategy for getting there, making sure it happens, and ensuring that people and property are protected against harm. Ministry is everything else: the daily, practical work of the congregation, including the rest of the decisions that must be made about what to do and how.

In thinking about organizational structures, people often use charts. The most common kind of "organization chart" uses boxes and lines to show who is in charge of whom. Organization charts have their uses, but to reconceive governance and ministry from the ground up, we need something a little different: a conceptual map. An organization chart traces lines of power and control; a conceptual map like the one in figure 4.1 shows how the various kinds of decisions an organization needs to make relate to one another. The map differentiates the roles of leaders, showing how they share in developing decisions while maintaining boundaries and remembering who will be consulted and who will make decisions on every subject.

Figure 4.1

GOVERNANCE AND MINISTRY

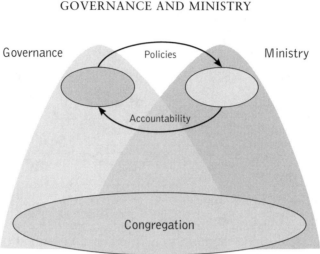

Figure 4.1 shows governance and ministry as two overlapping curves that together define three zones: at the left, governance; at the right, ministry; and in the middle, a zone of overlap for work shared by the two. At the top of each curve is its most frequent decision maker—typically the board for governance, the staff for ministry. By "staff" I mean to include clergy and other paid staff and also volunteers when they are functioning as leaders or workers in the congregation's daily ministry.

For the sake of simplicity, I will use the terms "board" and "staff" (or "ministry leaders") to designate the heads of these two loci of decision making, but in the diagram I'm leaving the top spots unlabeled for the moment, to recognize that congregations fill them differently. What healthy structures have in common is a clear understanding about the pathway to be followed when various decisions need to be made—who needs to be involved, who needs to express an opinion, and where each buck will stop. Depending on the subject matter, final decisions are made at the crest of one curve or the other.

(Note that "final" may not mean "ultimate." In most systems, both the governing board and ministry leaders work for one or more common bosses: the congregation, the presbytery, the conference, or the bishop. In a true organization chart, such entities would properly appear at the top. But this map shows only the governance/ministry subsystem, not the entire structure of congregational authority.)

Governance and ministry do not function in isolation from each other. They connect in several clearly defined ways:

- *First,* as mentioned, there is a zone of overlap at the bottom center of the diagram for issues that need input from both governance and ministry before traveling upward to the right or left for a decision. The distinction becomes sharper at the point of decision—at the top of each curve. Below these summits, the atmosphere is denser, more collaborative. Clear decision-making authority at the top actually makes it easier to share information, power, and influence throughout the organization.

- *Second,* the governing board connects with ministry leaders by adopting policies to guide their work. These policies include mission and vision statements, annual goals and budgets, and rules about finance, personnel, real estate, personal safety, and so on. Through policies, the governing board (which legally could make nearly every decision itself) delegates authority to ministry leaders and gives them guidance about how that authority should be used. In effect, the board sets a limit to its own agenda—deciding in advance that it will focus on its governance role, instead of trying to duplicate or supplant the work of ministry leaders in the daily management of congregational life.

- *Third,* the governing board holds the staff accountable. Responsible boards match delegated power with accountability—neither writing a blank check to ministry leaders nor holding them responsible for a result without first giving adequate authority to accomplish it. Having delegated power responsibly, the board monitors the work through regular reports and sees that individual performance is evaluated regularly. Accountability begins at home: no one step a board can take instills a spirit of accountability throughout the congregation more effectively than instituting regular evaluation of its own performance.

At the bottom of the picture is the congregation—not because it is less powerful than the others, but because its members serve in all three zones. As the diagram suggests, the distinction between governance and ministry is more important to leaders than to members. Most members do not need to think about the difference between governance and ministry at all.

A Wall of Separation

Some nonprofit organizations use the image of a "wall of separation" between board and staff, so that the board can focus on its function without being drawn into daily program management, and staff members are free from the distraction of board meddling. Figure 4.2 depicts this plan. In organizations that work this way, one hears, "Board members should never talk with staff without the executive director's knowledge and approval," or "The board decides what to do, and the staff does it." This structure has some merit, especially in a setting where the constituencies are easily separated. In a secular nonprofit—say, a mental-health clinic in a poor neighborhood—there is typically little or no overlap between board, staff, and clients. It would be rare to find that the executive director was counseling someone whose parent was on the board or that a major donor was also a staff member. When such multiple relationships are rare, it is possible to treat them as "role conflicts" or "conflicts of interest"—problems to be solved. When they are common, as in congregations, they need to be managed

Figure 4.2
"WALL OF SEPARATION"

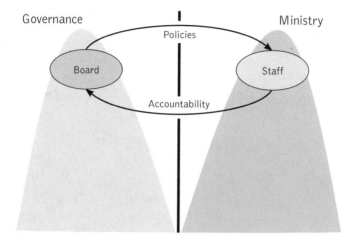

openly and ethically, but they cannot be eliminated. Conventional nonprofit wisdom needs to be examined and adjusted to fit congregational realities. Multiple relationships in congregations can be a source of problems, but they are a side effect of the fact that congregations, almost alone among the institutions of society, bring people together from a wide range of ages, occupations, and life situations. It is a good thing, not bad, that in congregations donors, workers, managers, and customers join at the board table for the work of governance.

Wearing Different Hats

Strict division of roles would also deprive congregational boards of necessary leadership from clergy and staff members as they discern the congregation's mission and decide on its direction. Most congregations would be hard hit if they had to separate the board so far from ministry as to deprive themselves of the voluntary labor of their board members in program and administration.

Too strict a rule against board "micromanagement" can prevent a board from learning firsthand about the congregation's work. Healthy congregations maintain firm boundaries about what decisions ultimately are made in which part of the structure, while at the same time encouraging continual interaction and collaboration across structural boundaries.

In place of the image of a wall or a strict division, a better metaphor for governance and ministry in congregations involves hats. Each hat represents a different kind of activity: a board member has a board hat, but if he's a tenor in the choir, he takes his board hat off and wears his choir hat to rehearsals. The change may help to remind him that board membership confers no musical authority: if the director says he's out of tune, he's out of tune! A board member who happens to be the leader of a ministry activity takes the ministry hat off to serve as an unbiased guarantor of the whole mission, not a representative of just one aspect. Congregations may try for the strict separation sometimes advocated in other nonprofits, but it's difficult because, especially in small and midsize congregations, people wear so many hats. The larger the congregation, the more useful it is to separate governance and ministry in time and space, with different (but still overlapping) groups of people and with different leaders at the helm. Even in the largest congregations, it is both impossible and undesirable to sever governance from ministry entirely, and so the metaphor of hats can be a useful reminder that each role has a separate set of duties.

The most desirable relation between governance and ministry is partnership, and partnership depends on both clear boundaries and a relationship of mutual support. A board that overemphasizes its role as a watchdog can induce its ministry workers—paid and unpaid—to draw their wagons into circles or (switching metaphors) to fly below the radar, achieving autonomy by hiding information. On the other hand, a clergy leader who "manages" the board so deftly that it loses its ability to push back and question clergy leadership turns the congregation into a one-legged stool, unstable because its base of leadership depends too much on one person. In evaluating various ways of organizing, it is good to ask, "Does this structure create boundaries between roles that are firm but permeable so the parties can approach each other as independent and cooperating partners?"

Clearer Definitions

Now that we've seen the overview, it's time to define governance and ministry more formally.

Governance means "owning" the congregation, exercising ultimate control of its human and material resources and ensuring that it serves its mission. The *mission* is not the same as a mission *statement*—though stating the mission afresh from time to time is a central responsibility of governance. The mission is what mission statements try to state. Even the best mission statement is an approximation, subject to improvement or revision as new light dawns and circumstances change. Good mission statements make clear what good the congregation means to do, whom it hopes to benefit and how, and what it claims as its central principles or values. Articulating mission is a central role of governance. Major choices about goals and strategies also belong to governance, as does deciding who will be responsible for implementing them. Governance requires delegating power to those who direct the daily work, and holding them accountable for their performance. Governance means seeing that the congregation's money, property, and people are kept safe, and that the congregation lives in harmony with its own values. Governance connects the congregation's work with the concerns of various stakeholders: its members, future members, donors, and volunteers; its wider community; its family of related congregations; and its ancestors in faith—the honored dead who are its greater "cloud of witnesses." Governance is holding the whole institution and its work in trust, voicing its intentions, making its biggest decisions, and taking responsibility for its performance.

Ministry is most of the rest of what a congregation does— achieving the inward and outward results the congregation exists to achieve. Anyone whose job it is to lead a program, teach a class, serve food, lead worship, or help visitors to find a seat is part of ministry. So are people who provide indirect support by training others, writing checks, sweeping floors, and tuning the piano. In using the word ministry, I do not distinguish between ordained and lay, paid and unpaid, or "program" and "administrative" staff. Anyone who is part of the chain of practical activities that constitute a congregation's work I count as part of its ministry. Ministry includes creating liturgies, curricula, visitation schedules, and countless other long- and short-term plans. Ministry means making daily choices about money, time, and space. If ministry is to be more than a one-man or one-woman show, it also requires writing job descriptions, setting goals, conducting evaluations, hiring staff members, and sometimes firing them. Ministry, to put it simply, is the active, "doing" aspect of the congregation.

A simple way to see the difference between governance and ministry is by the results each kind of work produces. Both governance and ministry, ideally, produce relationships, enthusiasm, and renewed faith. But each also generates a distinctive set of outcomes: Governance produces minutes, policies, mission statements, goals, and strategic-planning documents. Ministry brings into being worship services, study groups, mission trips, service projects, mowed lawns, happy children, and renewed hope. One too-simple summary might be that governance produces words on paper, and ministry produces action. The reality is only a bit more complicated.

Another way of seeing the difference between governance and ministry is to picture the type of group that does each best. Effective governance most typically requires diverse, representative groups of people who sit around tables having orderly discussion.

Now and then they may break into smaller groups to make sure everyone's ideas are heard and considered. Procedure is formal enough to make it clear when the group as a whole has endorsed something and exactly what it has endorsed. Somebody takes minutes, and when a decision has been made and written down, the essential work of governance is done. The best group for doing governance is diverse, patient, verbal, and at ease with abstract thinking and intangible work products.

The most effective group—or team—for doing ministry is different in almost every way. First, a ministry team needs to be *un*representative: it systematically excludes everyone who lacks commitment to the task at hand. A ministry group begins with at least general clarity about the work to be done. It needs a leader who knows how to do it and is willing to accept responsibility for training, supervising, and coordinating others to achieve a stated goal. Unlike governing bodies, which are usually elected, the selection of ministry groups is based on people's passion for the goal, with an eye to making sure group members have among them the gifts and time the ministry will need.

Teams doing ministry can and should make many decisions about how and what to do, whether they receive clear guidance from a governing body or not. In many congregations the most top-down style of leadership is found in the choir, where directors actually direct! But even choirs pause periodically during rehearsals to discuss whether they wish they were singing different music. Sometimes the director accommodates such preferences—not because it is more democratic for the choir to choose the music (the director may, in fact, have a better sense of the choir's capabilities, what's appropriate for the day or season, and what kind of music the congregation likes), but because empowered groups have more enthusiasm and more energy than passive ones. The essential qualities of an effective ministry team, in contrast to a governing body, are passion, urgency, unity, problem-solving skills, and a preference for action over talk.

The difference between governance and ministry is *not* hard versus soft, money versus faith, top versus bottom, or business versus people. Both governance and ministry concern themselves with faith and values, both involve prayer and study, and both require decisions about how to deploy financial, capital, and human resources for the congregation's purposes.

Governance and ministry do not absolutely need to be done by different people, at different times, or under different leadership. It is quite possible to gather one group to do both these things, as most committees in committee-centered congregations try to do. But even in the smallest congregation, where the same twelve people seem to do everything, the distinction between governance and ministry can be of value, if only to help leaders to shift gears efficiently.

Who Plays the Roles?

In figure 4.1, I left the governance and ministry decision-maker bubbles unfilled. In some congregations, deciding how to fill these bubbles is the most difficult part of clarifying the decision-making structure. What are the options?

Governance most frequently is the responsibility of a board, and ministry is led by an ordained clergyperson—but this general statement touches neither the variety of ways congregations actually organize nor the complexity of the daily dance within a given structure. The board-centered structure described in chapter 3 vests the board with responsibility for both governance and ministry; in a small congregation this arrangement has benefits. The committee-centered structure mixes governance and ministry at every point, and in the process often creates a structure that has a hard time either saying what it means to do, or doing it. This confusion is especially likely to arise when the congregation gets too large to manage its relationships informally. The staff-centered structure achieves efficiency by handing governance and ministry to one person, in effect sacrificing congregational democracy on the altar of efficiency. The "wall of separation" model commonly espoused in the nonprofit world clearly distinguishes governance from ministry (or management)—so clearly, in fact, as to feel a bit stiff and artificial even in a secular nonprofit. In congregations, the idea of strict separation is an amusing concept, but not a practical or desirable plan because mixed roles are so ubiquitous. In the end, each congregation needs to strike its own balance between democracy and efficiency, tradition and change, clarity and informality. Congregations that belong to some larger family (as virtually all do, including those called "nondenominational") must also decide how much they will conform to the organizational patterns of the larger group. These complexities are important, and they deserve prayerful thought. The three indispensable requirements of organizational effectiveness, in my view, are that a congregation have a unified structure for making governance decisions; a unified structure for making ministry decisions; and a firm boundary, with active mutual communication and accountability, between them.

Any structure a congregation agrees upon that meets all three of these requirements is likely to offer a significant increase in its capacity to set a course and to travel swiftly and harmoniously toward the fulfillment of its mission.

The Governance Decision Maker

The most important governance decision maker almost always is a board. Most boards share governance authority with another body or individual—the congregation, presbytery, bishop, or Mother Church. If the board is "advisory" to the clergy leader, whether intentionally (as in Roman Catholic parishes) or because the board has a low concept of its governance responsibilities, then the clergy leader becomes, by default, the governance decision maker. Some congregations, as I've mentioned, have several boards, each of which is the top governance decision maker in a certain sphere. I don't think this is a particularly good idea, but it happens. In many congregations, perhaps even the majority, no one really fills the governance decision-maker role. The result tends to be a church divided into "silos," with good people doing good things in each of them, but with little sense of overall direction, difficulty responding clearly and consistently to inappropriate behavior, and heavy—if often unacknowledged—dependence on clergy leaders to maintain morale and generate a sense of vision.

Traditional Quaker meetings ask their members to participate in governance through direct congregational dialogue and consensus building. To achieve this level of participation, Quakers require high commitment from their members—far beyond what most Jews, or most other Christians, would accept. Some congregational-polity churches want to have this cake and eat it, too—refusing to delegate significant power to the board or staff without asking the whole membership to spend the time and energy to do a good job of direct decision making. The result is that no one has the power or responsibility to make significant decisions—hence no significant decisions get made, and by default the winner is the status quo.

Congregations that successfully revise their structure to be more responsive and adaptive most frequently choose to assign governance authority to a board of six to eight. Such a board is small enough to engage in serious discernment work and so small that it should be obvious to everyone that it can't legitimately do its work in isolation. The congregation exercises its control not by making many small decisions but by making a few large ones well. An essential part of the board's responsibility is to choose wisely which few subjects merit congregational attention, and to host a rich, reflective dialogue among the members on those subjects.

The Ministry Decision Maker

Who should be the ministry decision maker? In most congregations with an active membership of more than two hundred children and adults, the most straightforward solution is to delegate day-to-day decision making to the senior minister or rabbi. In large congregations, senior clergy will in turn delegate authority to other staff members to make decisions in their spheres. Senior clergy who stand apart from day-to-day administration may prefer to have just one person reporting to them—an administrative number two, to whom all other staff report. For obvious reasons this arrangement is usually practicable only in larger congregations, and it requires complete trust between the two top staff people.

In practice, many issues are decided collaboratively, through ad hoc conversation or in staff meetings. Congregations with a strong commitment to egalitarian, collaborative leadership sometimes prefer to delegate ministry decision making to a team of staff, or of staff and lay leaders, rather than to an individual. Such arrangements call for an ongoing investment in team building.

Another option often chosen by congregations that resist concentrating too much power in the hands of the clergy leader is to create a many-headed structure for ministry. Many synagogues, for instance, have two operational "heads" reporting to the board—the rabbi for things spiritual and an executive director for financial and property matters. Sometimes boards—usually without intending to—create a hydra-headed structure with a half-dozen or more department heads with no clear accountability within the staff. Such structures sometimes work—but I suspect that their success owes more to the personalities involved than to the merits of the structure.

There are many options for assigning ministry authority, but congregations that address this issue thoughtfully most often choose a simple head-of-staff model, perhaps softened by a stated expectation that the head of staff will lead in a consultative, collegial manner. The difficulty with more complicated schemes is rooted in a basic principle of administration: anyone who supervises someone else needs to devote enough time to do it well, and the amount of time required grows more quickly than the number of people supervised. The more lines of accountability that run to the board, the more time the board and its leaders will spend directing work, mediating differences, and making decisions that fall through the inevitable cracks.

To misquote both John Donne and Harry Truman: "Ask not with whom the buck stops; it stops with thee." If the board does not clearly designate who will make decisions, it can plan on making them itself. Since boards usually hope to spend more time governing and less time managing, they generally create a single structure for ministry with a single head, empower that person to decide management questions, and hold him or her accountable for the performance of the staff.

Figure 4.3
COMMITTEES AND TEAMS

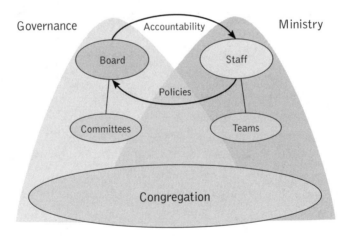

Committees and Teams

Both board and staff need helpers, but because their jobs are different, they need helpers organized in different ways. Figure 4.3 distinguishes committees, reporting to the board, and teams, reporting to the staff. Many congregations call both kinds of groups "committees," but I prefer to use the word in the more traditional sense of a group to which a deliberative body has referred, or "committed," a piece of business. A committee gathers information, drafts a policy, or prepares in some other way to report back to the body that appointed it. In a board-centered congregation, where the board's job is to manage as well as to govern, some committees mow the lawn, arrange flowers, or visit the sick. Even in that case, though, "committee" is a silly name for the gang that shows up Saturday with greasy coveralls and pipe wrenches. Requiring members of that gang to sit around a table, adopt motions, and keep minutes is even sillier; berating them for being "not really a committee" if they fail to practice the committee niceties is downright self-defeating.

True Committees and Task Forces

A board that undertakes to govern, especially when it has a history of managing, is wise to keep its committees separate from the groups that carry out the work of ministry—and giving them a different name is one way to make the difference clear. A true governing board has few committees, and most of them are temporary. Ad hoc committees might draft policies or gather data, so that the board can have a good conversation about some aspect of the congregation's mission, or about some other policy question. A board concerned primarily with governance would not appoint a committee to look into changing the locks or to help the religious educator run the Sunday school, because those tasks fall into the zone of ministry. A governing board has ultimate responsibility for securing the building, but it discharges that responsibility best when it delegates adequate authority to manage the building, states clearly how secure it wants the building to be, and then holds its delegate accountable for the result. If a group of volunteers does the actual work (and in most congregations, who else would do it?) a better name is "team."

By this strict definition, what committees might a board have? It certainly should have a governance committee to recruit and train new board members and help the board to maintain high standards of performance. It probably needs a finance committee, though the scope of the committee's work should hew to the same limits the board sets for its own finance-related work. (I'll have more to say about financial management and budgeting in later chapters; suffice it to say now that for the board to create committees to "help" the staff carry out responsibilities the board has delegated to the staff is a first step backward down the slope to triangulation and gridlock. Finances are central to the board's fiduciary role, of course—but to fulfill that role effectively, the board needs to discipline itself not to step into the small fiscal potatoes, and its committees need to do the same.) True committees, by definition, help the board do the board's work, and conversely, any work the board assigns to a committee remains part of the board's job description. Consequently most committees should be temporary, appointed in light of the immediate exigencies of board business. An ad hoc committee might draft bylaw amendments, study a proposed building project, or prepare for board reflection on an ethical question that the board might want to make a policy about. Another name for an ad hoc committee is "task force."

In exceptional cases, a board might delegate the oversight of a certain function—an endowment fund, a nursery school, or the construction of a new sanctuary—to a standing committee. A nursery-school director, for instance, might report to a committee that is, in effect, a school board that reports in turn to the congregation's board. An endowment fund might have a management committee that reports to the board but not to the head of staff, to reduce the temptation of entrusting both the conservation and the use of an endowment to the same person. These arrangements can be useful, though a board should be careful in creating them, lest it spend too much of its precious time managing a proliferating band of sub-boards. By delegating management decision making in a specific area to a committee, the board makes itself the CEO in that realm.

When possible, the board should keep ad hoc committees and task forces on a short leash, requiring them to come back to the board regularly and to complete their work on a short time line. Committees' job is to help the board, not to take its place. A good ad hoc committee sets the stage for a well-informed board conversation and decision; a poor one makes its own decision and then dares the board to overturn it "after we did all that work."

Teams

Committees write reports, make recommendations, and gather information. Teams, on the other hand, produce practical results. Some teams directly fulfill pieces of the congregation's mission, producing the primary results the mission calls for. Worship teams, educational ministries; outreach, service, and social-action teams; hospitality and caring teams; and choirs—depending how the congregation sees its mission—fall into the primary-results category. Other teams (or the same teams on a different day) produce supportive, secondary results: a clean building, a fund-drive mailing, a readable newsletter, an attractive garden. And of course all of them, potentially, invite people into mutually supportive and inspiring friendships, which through the power of good example may do more to transform lives than intentional life-changing programs do.

One benefit of separating governance from ministry is that ministry teams can serve without the extra burden of too wide a scope of decision making. Every team will make decisions—one sound principle of management is that a team should take as much responsibility for choosing *how* to do its work as it can handle. But there is no reason why someone with a heart for child care needs to attend meetings to interpret the insurance company requirements about child safety—or vice versa. Separating governance from ministry also frees ministry from some of the limits to its growth. Committees in committee-centered congregations often act as gatekeepers, limiting initiative within a given area. "We have our hands full. In fact, we have trouble filling our committee as it is. How can we possibly take on something else?" A team structure, responsible to staff, is more expandable: one staff person can oversee a dozen teams, and a volunteer might support two or three. Together they would be responsible for the activities of some two hundred active individuals.

Teams free congregations from the limitations of the "Map Theory of Committees" (see chapter 3). A congregation with six good ideas for new-member outreach need not squeeze them all through one swamped membership committee. It can recruit six leaders to recruit six teams charged with just one idea each. A good rule is never to start a team whose name begins with "*the*": *the* choir, *the* youth group, *the* social-ministry team, *the* women's fellowship. Such names announce, right from the start, that there will never be another. The old practice of naming women's circles and adult classes after their leaders has its own problems, but it at least holds out the possibility that there might someday be one named for someone else! Unique names ("Jubilee Singers," "Vance," "Daughters of Esther") work against this one-and-only style of thinking, opening the door to multiple points of entry for people of all kinds and interests.

The Congregation

What, then, is the role of the congregation? Figure 4.5 shows the congregation spread across the bottom of the map, playing three distinct roles: As *governors,* members of the congregation meet to play a formal, corporate decision-making role. The exact nature of that role varies. The congregation may be the supreme organ of governance, as in a congregational-polity church, or it may share

Figure 4.4
ROLES OF THE CONGREGATION

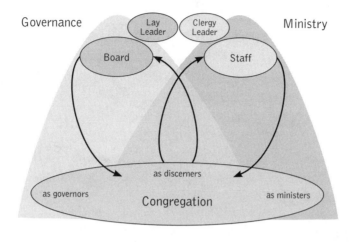

that role with the larger denominational family, as in presbyterian and episcopal systems. In the United States, the congregation plays a powerful role in virtually every congregation; it may vote with hands and voices, or mainly with its feet and pocketbooks—but vote it does, and leaders do well to pay attention.

The right side of the diagram shows the congregation's role as *ministers*. As volunteers, members of the congregation are the main labor pool for ministry. Heavy dependence on unpaid labor is a distinctive challenge of congregational leadership, and the increasingly high expectations of volunteer workers are a distinctive challenge of our time. Every congregation has good workers who rarely come to meetings—in effect, one congregation governs while another does the work! Many gifts—as Paul might say—but that's OK so long as there's one spirit.

In the middle of the diagram is a third role for the members of the congregation: as *discerners*. When members contribute to strategic planning, or participate in vision sessions, or attend town meetings called by the board to discuss unanswered questions about mission, they are acting as discerners. Discernment aims to discover what good the congregation truly exists to do—what part of God's will is ours to accomplish. It is as discerners that the board and staff engage the congregation in continual "holy conversation."[1] The arrows leading to and from the congregation as discerners represent this conversation.

Members readily see the difference between working in a soup kitchen (ministry), voting at a meeting (governance), and reflecting in small groups about the implications for the congregation of neighborhood change (discernment). Members play other, non-organizational roles as well—as receivers of service, worshipers, students, and evangelists. But usually they flow from one role to another without thinking much about it. The roles of governance and ministry are most distinct, and self-discipline about observing boundaries most important, at the top of the diagram, where board and staff live.

Most members of the congregation see the difference between governance and ministry best when it is symbolized in the relationship between the most visible ministry and governance leaders. Typically these are the senior clergy leader and the top lay leader: rabbi and president, pastor and board chair, rector and senior warden, or—in some Presbyterian churches—minister and clerk of session. Quite apart from the specific roles and powers assigned to these positions, the relationship between the people who hold them can enhance a congregation's sense of harmony and organizational well-being.

Four Leadership Roles

Figure 4.5 presents a summary of the whole pattern of relationships described in this chapter. The work of governance and ministry is shown distributed among four major areas of work: oversight, strategy, discernment, and management.[2]

Figure 4.5
ROLES OF BOARD AND STAFF

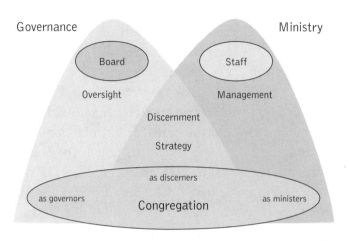

1. *Oversight* belongs to the board, which maintains a certain separation from the staff in order to maintain sufficient objectivity to serve as an effective check and balance.

2. *Management* is the staff's sphere—here, too, some separation and clear boundaries need to be in place. The staff accepts responsibility for managing its own internal relationships and for using the authority it has been delegated. A staff that continually seeks approval or permission from the board diminishes its own effectiveness and robs time from the board's real work.

3. *Discernment and strategy.* In the shared zone in the middle of the diagram are *discernment*—articulating mission and vision—and *strategy*: making the big choices about capital investments, staffing, program philosophy, and outreach goals. No matter who plays the final decision-making role in these two areas, the process leading up to a decision needs to be a shared one.

Some boards say, "We decide the mission, and the staff carries it out." But this division of labor is far from the reality in congregations, where clergy and staff play a strong leadership role in the discernment process. Nor does it make sense, in my view, to insist rigidly that the head of staff make "means" decisions on his or her own, and that the board confine itself to writing abstract "ends" policies and a priori prohibitions on staff action. A congregation thinking about moving across town or building a new building or inviting a new ethnic group to its worship services needs to strive together toward such choices, and the members need both lay and professional leaders striving with them. The quality of the process and the conversation matters much more than the technicality of who makes the final decision, because such choices can succeed only with broad support. The next three chapters discuss in more detail the roles of board and staff, and how they can work as strong, well-differentiated partners.

There is no one right way to organize a congregation; each community of faith must choose a structure right for its own values and beliefs, and in harmony with the practice of its historic tradition and its larger family of congregations. What too many congregations choose, however, is a loose, ambiguous structure that creates a strong, unwanted bias against change. If the world were stable and the religious needs of people stayed the same from one generation to the next, that might be fine. But in the world as it is, congregations that persist at practices that worked in generations past find themselves in slow decline. Among those practices are the board-centered and committee-centered modes of governance that emerged early in the 1900s. In their place, congregations are experimenting with alternatives. The most successful of these efforts focus strongly on the congregation's mission— rather than on organizational life for its own sake. They also have in common clarity about the difference between governance and ministry, clarity about which buck stops where and how leaders will be held accountable. Equipped with a clear structure, such congregations can identify their mission clearly, choose a strategy, get out from under their own feet, and move ahead.

5 :: The Job of the Board

As a conversation starter, sometimes I ask board members to tell me what their job is. I hear a variety of answers. Someone usually says, "We represent the members of the congregation. They elected us, and we should do what they would do." The board, in this political perspective, is like a city council or the U.S. Congress: representatives elected by the people to make law in their behalf. The comparison is not new: civil government and congregations have exerted mutual influence in North America since colonial times. In our national tradition, "we the people" exercise our sovereignty through representatives, and so Americans tend to assume congregations should be organized that way as well. But "doing what the people who elected us would do" is no simpler for a board than for a legislator. Should a board do what its constituents want, or what they *would* want if they understood the issues better and had spent more time thinking more deeply about long-term implications? A problem with democracy in congregations (and elsewhere) is that future voters do not vote. If they did, at every meeting and election they would make up a majority—we hope! Since most congregations plan to be around for more than a short time, the board must represent not only current members but the disenfranchised future also. Clearly, this responsibility requires an understanding of the board's job that goes deeper than "we represent the members."

Board members sometimes say, "Our job is to give the members what they want." This idea depicts members of the congregation as customers and the congregation as a store. The customer is king, and the chief end of the congregation is to please the customer. Higher motives may exist alongside this one—a store owner may have other motives than to make a profit—but the board's overriding motivation is to keep the congregation voting "yes" with both its dollars and its feet. The key metrics of success are quantitative: membership, attendance, contributions, and participation. This perspective on the board's job explains quite a lot of what an effective board does—especially when it pays attention to the changing culture, tastes, and demographics of its service area, and leads the congregation to refresh its program and recharge its appeal. But is this really the point of a congregation? Congregations do some of their best work when, instead of giving people what they want, they teach them to want something new. It is not unusual to hear a person thank a congregation for the fact that he or she now volunteers to help the needy or takes risks for social justice. Sometimes a congregant abandons a job that is just a job, at some sacrifice of income, in favor of a morally significant vocation. When people talk about such profound life changes, I sometimes ask, "What would you have done if someone warned you how belonging to this congregation would transform your life?" Often they admit they would have run the other way. The idea of "giving the members what they want" fails to grasp the value of a congregation that intends to influence, not simply to reflect, its members' preferences and values.

A third answer I occasionally hear is, "We are ministers alongside the pastor." This is a powerful idea, personified in Reformed theology as the ruling elder, ordained to lead along with teaching elders, also known as pastors. In current Presbyterian practice, ruling elders are elected and serve terms like most other board members, but the rite of ordination (and the lasting honorary status it confers) makes ruling elders more than simple representatives. Elders, as one scholar put it, rule "according to the guidance of their own nurtured consciences and not merely as spokespersons of particular interest groups."[1] While not so explicit in most non-Reformed traditions, the idea that a lay board member's work is a form of ministry is worth considering in any congregation. Making a board member part of the congregation's ordained leadership recognizes "gifts of the spirit" in the individual, and acknowledges that boards sometimes need to lead constituent opinion rather than reflect it.

While the idea of board-member-as-minister deepens our understanding of an individual board member's role, it does less to clarify the work of the board itself. A board is not simply the sum of its members. It has a role to play and products to turn out collectively. In order to work happily and in harmony, board members need to know with some precision what role they are to play and what results they should produce.

The Board as Fiduciary

Sometimes when I ask, "What is the board's job?" someone (frequently a lawyer or a banker) uses an obscure word that speaks rather deeply to the nature of the board's role: "The board is a fiduciary." And what might a fiduciary be? Many people connect this word exclusively with money, but the concept actually is much broader. A fiduciary (in Latin, *fiduciarius*, "trust," from *fides*, "faith") is anyone whose duty is to act in faithfulness to the interest of another, even at cost or peril to himself. A parent, for example, is a fiduciary for his or her children and must care for them, no matter how much sacrifice that might require. The stewards in Jesus's parables, who managed the master's property while he was absent, were fiduciaries. The board of a business corporation holds the corporate assets as fiduciary for the stockholders. Since the stockholders' main interest, ordinarily, is to make money, the duty of a corporate board is to increase stockholder value. If the board seeks other goals—by pumping up executive compensation, making sweetheart deals with other companies owned by board members, or sometimes even trying to be responsible corporate citizens—they can expect to be accused of failing as fiduciaries.

A congregation's board is a fiduciary, also. Like a for-profit board, it controls property in behalf of its real owner. But who is the owner? Who owns a church? Who owns a synagogue? Often board members answer this question too quickly: "The members are the owners!" And the owners' interest? Satisfactory worship, education, social action, and so on. The fiduciary duty of a congregation's board, in this view, is to know what the congregation wants and to provide it—a concept not so different from the political and commercial concepts of the board described above. This way of thinking sometimes produces good results, but it is based on a false assumption. A congregation does exist to serve its owner—but the members of a nonprofit corporation do not "own" it as stockholders own a business. Corporate stockholders can vote to liquidate the corporation's property, pay its debts, and divide the proceeds among themselves. A congregation—or any other nonprofit—that did likewise would be violating several state and federal laws. The most fundamental legal principle of nonprofit corporations is that they must use their resources exclusively for the specific purposes for which the state has chartered them. In the case of congregations, the charter purposes are relatively broad. For that reason, and because a congregation is exempt from many of the tax reports required of other charities, it is easy to forget that there is any limitation at all. But a congregation may not distribute its resources for the "personal benefit" of anyone—especially an officer or board member—except as reimbursement of expenses or fair compensation for services provided. For-profit corporations are required to benefit their stockholders, while nonprofits are forbidden to benefit their members. To call the members "owners" under these conditions stretches the idea of ownership quite far.

Owned by the Mission

Who, then, is the owner of a congregation? Who plays the role of the stockholders in a business? Not the members. Not the board. Not the clergy or the bishop or the staff. All these are fiduciaries whose duty is to serve the owner. Symbolically, we might say God or Jesus is the owner, and that might be a correct interpretation. But the concept of God is too big to guide decision making helpfully. The "owner" that the board must serve is *this congregation's mission*, the small piece of God's will that belongs to it. Or to put it differently, the congregation's job is to find the mission it belongs to, the real owner for whose benefit the leaders hold and deploy resources. Any effort to improve the governance of a congregation begins by recognizing that its primary measure of success is not the balance in the bank, the shortness of board meetings, or the happiness of congregants. A congregation's "bottom line" is the degree to which its mission is achieved. The mission, like stockholders in a business, has the moral right both to control the congregation's actions and to benefit from them. Because the match between a congregation's mission and a corporation's stockholders is so close, it seems to me helpful to say that the owner of a congregation is its mission.[2]

An interesting corollary of this line of thought is that when members of the congregation vote, they, too, are fiduciaries for the mission. When a member's interests conflict with the congregation's mission, the member's duty is to vote the mission. Like the board, each member has a duty to make sure the congregation serves its mission—to vote as a fiduciary for the owner—even if that goes against the member's private preferences or wishes.

And what is the mission? The great management consultant Peter Drucker wrote that the core product of all social-sector organizations is "a changed human being."[3] A congregation's mission is its unique answer to the question, "Whose lives do we intend to change and in what way?" A congregation that limits its vision to pleasing its members falls short of its true purpose. Growth, expanding budgets, building programs, and such trappings of success matter only if they reflect positive transformation in the lives of the people touched by the congregation's work.

Fiduciary Duties of Board Members

As fiduciaries for the mission, individual board members have certain legal duties: the duty of care, the duty of loyalty, and the duty of obedience.

The *duty of care* requires that a board member commit adequate time, energy, and attention to enable him or her to know the mission, understand the congregation's affairs, and act responsibly. One way to look at this obligation is to ask, "If I personally owned the congregation—its property, its money, and its program—how much time would I devote to managing it? How well would I feel I needed to understand its finances? What kind of assurance would I need that it was well insured, that no one was stealing from it, and that my money was being put to the intended use?" No one board member will understand everything the board needs to understand—but each board member is separately responsible for taking "reasonable care" in governing the congregation. Taking care means that a board member who does not understand financial statements needs to seek out someone who can help decipher them, so that he or she can find the answers to the few key questions of greatest concern to the board. Board members unfamiliar with important program areas need to seek out at least a basic understanding of how each area of ministry supports the mission. The board as a whole can help with this kind of learning by orienting new board members and allotting time periodically for the whole board to refresh its knowledge. The ultimate responsibility for taking care remains, however, with the individual board member.

Specifically, the duty of care requires thorough preparation for board meetings, regular attendance, and active participation. It also means voting when it is appropriate to vote. On some boards, "abstentions" have become so customary that the minutes show a count of zero abstentions when there are none. Abstentions are appropriate or even required in certain circumstances, as when a member has a clear conflict of interest, but otherwise a board member who does not vote is failing to perform a duty. The congregation has a board to govern its affairs, and the duty of care requires every board member to understand the issues and to cast the vote with which he or she has been entrusted. Members who abstain should be asked to give a reason why. In many cases people abstain to reserve the right to undermine the board's decision later—not an appropriate reason or appropriate behavior for board members.

A board member owes the congregation a *duty of loyalty*. This means first of all that for a board member one consideration must be paramount—the congregation's mission. Most obviously, a board member who stands to benefit, personally or through a close relationship, from a decision of the board must promptly disclose the conflict of interest. If the conflict is significant, the board member must withdraw, not only from voting but from discussions leading to a vote. In response to recent abuses in the nonprofit sector, the IRS has begun to pay increased attention to conflicts of interest among nonprofit board members. While legal consequences for individual board members are still rare, a board that does not handle conflicts of interest properly risks costly "intermediate sanctions" against the congregation, not to mention criticism or even lawsuits from anyone who claims to have been harmed by a biased board decision.

The duty of loyalty extends beyond legal conflicts of interest. Personal preferences, friendships, rivalries, and bitterness from past divisions can cloud the objectivity of any board member. When the board is set up to have "representatives" from program areas, such biases can be exacerbated or even made to seem legitimate. These kinds of conflicts usually can be handled simply, by candid acknowledgment of them and shared understanding that board members' duty is to set aside all partial loyalties in favor of the whole.

While the duty of loyalty is individual, wise boards have a written policy that defines conflicts of interest and requires board members to disclose them and to withdraw from debate and voting. A clear conflict-of-interest policy, in addition to protecting the church from harm, protects board members from unjust accusations. If the policy is fuzzy, a board member might vote, supposing in good faith that the conflict of interest involved is trivial or that the proposed action is so clearly in the church's favor that no one could find fault. But it is risky to assume that "no one could find fault." Someone always can, and someone often will. When board members resist writing a conflict-of-interest policy to protect the congregation, I sometimes suggest they write one to protect themselves.

The *duty of obedience* requires board members to comply with the congregation's foundational documents—which may include a charter, bylaws, and denominational rules—and applicable laws. Most important, board members must be obedient to the mission, even as they recast it in new mission statements from time to time. It is easy to confuse the happiness of influential individuals with the mission; board members need to be alert to times when the right action will make people *un*happy. The duty of loyalty is not to the congregation as a present group of individuals; it is to the mission.

Sometimes we speak of "this year's board" or "last year's board," as though each had a separate life. But a board, like the corporation it controls, is a continuing legal and moral entity. It inherits all the promises it has made, even if all individual board members are new. The board is the first guarantor of the congregation's good name and integrity; as such it must "obey" past promises, including written and unwritten contracts and donor restrictions it has accepted by accepting gifts. Even unilateral promises, though not always enforceable by law, are moral obligations to which a board should adhere if at all possible.

I was impressed, as a young person serving on a church board, when I saw my elders handling an awkward situation. In conversation with a ministerial candidate, the chair of the endowment committee said he "saw no problem" with lending the minister money for a down payment on a house, and added, "We can do that." He was a board member, but he had not been authorized to make such a commitment. Many boards would have apologized to the candidate and washed their hands of the matter. But one board member said, "If a person in a responsible position makes a promise for the church, we are obligated to make good on it." That was what the board did, and I believe it was correct to do so—if not legally, then morally.

This story also illuminates another aspect of the duty of obedience: board members have a duty to respect the limits of their individual role vis-à-vis the board as a whole. Board members scattered through the social hall after a service are not the board. They become the board only at a duly called board meeting, and the board acts only as a unit. Individual board members, as such, have no special rights or powers except to participate and vote at board meetings. At meetings, board members disagree sharply, but once a vote is taken, the duty of obedience requires every member to speak with respect of the decision and the board's authority to make it. Some boards carry this obligation further, and forbid members to disclose their disagreement to others in the congregation. I think this practice goes too far and violates the basic principle of openness about board business. But at the very least, a board member should say something like, "It was the board's responsibility to make this decision. I disagreed and said so, but we had a frank discussion and a vote, and now it is time to move ahead." If a board member's dissent is so strong that he or she cannot voice at least that level of support for the board's legitimate authority, then it is time to think about resigning.

The duties of care, loyalty, and obedience may seem almost too obvious to mention (so, incidentally, do about half of the Ten Commandments). But it is not in moments of reflection that we need a moral code to remind us of our duties. It is in heated moments, when it may seem reasonable to depart from the normal constraints, that code morality is helpful. These are exactly the times when a clear statement of the responsibilities of board members, and clear policies that spell out what to do when issues arise, become especially important. In extreme cases (typically, "gross negligence") board members may be held personally liable for actions of the board that violate the law or the foundational documents. Regular conversation about the legal duties of board members and a written covenant of board behavior are good ways to strengthen every member's native sense of what is right.

Governing by Policy

We move now from the duties of board members to the role of the board itself. One source of information on this subject is the foundational documents (charter, bylaws, canons, and denominational rulebooks) that define the purpose, powers, and duties of the board. Beyond their general statement of the board's purpose (which often is quite thoughtful) such documents often are not much help. Foundational documents typically preserve ideas about boards that belong to an earlier era. They also tend to overemphasize problems, because new provisions are more likely to be added during times of conflict. Over time, sections about how to address problems overwhelm those that describe healthy functioning. Foundational documents also naturally and appropriately focus on the legal aspects of a board's role, in particular on the extent and limits of its powers. Most boards have more power over congregational life than they possibly can use on their own.

Effective boards don't try. Instead they choose a few critical areas where the board's contribution is essential and unique—and delegate the rest. To focus its attention, a board has to put firm boundaries around its own agenda. It remains responsible for everything under its authority, but controls some things directly, shares control of others, and delegates yet others fully. To achieve this level of self-discipline a board needs a better-nuanced understanding of its role than foundational documents are likely to provide.

Figure 5.1
ROLES OF BOARD AND STAFF

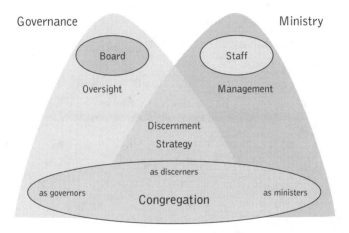

Our conceptual map (see figure 5.1) divides the board's sphere of influence into zones by whether the board takes responsibility for them directly (oversight), shares them (strategy and discernment), or delegates them (management). Effective boards adopt clear policies to govern all of these zones, but each zone requires a different type of policy. We will discuss how a board's policies address each zone in turn, but first we need to define "policy."

A policy is an authoritative written statement designed to control many individual decisions over time. Ineffective boards sit and receive business items brought by individual board members, staff, or others, and decide, one at time, each case. Some boards actually assume that any member of the congregation has a right to put an item on the board's agenda. A board that operates this way is apt to have long, frustrating meetings, with little to show for them at year's end. Policies provide the framework for decisions to be made away from the board table.

Board policies must be consistent with the bylaws and other foundational documents. Sometimes it is tempting to repeat or restate what the bylaws say already for the sake of having a complete rulebook, "all in one place." I would advise against such repetition, because it can create confusion to have two versions of the same rule. It is better to refer to related bylaws in the text of a policy, and then to keep a copy of the bylaws handy.

Many boards believe they are making policy when they actually are setting precedents. Like medieval kings sitting as courts of last resort, they receive petitions and decide cases. Anyone who has a complaint or does not like a decision made elsewhere in the organization can come to the board and hope for better. Over time, the board loses much of its power to initiate action and becomes reactive, giving and withholding assent to propositions brought to it by others. One way for a board to escape from this reactive position is to insist on spending its time making policy instead of deciding cases. A board that intends to govern by policy will question the appropriateness of any matter on its agenda that controls only a single event.

A few one-time decisions are so wide-reaching in their implications—moving to a new location or making a major change in program emphasis, for example—that almost any board would choose to make them rather than delegate them. But such decisions are not common. Any agenda item that would control only a one-time event should prompt the board to ask: "Does this decision have such wide or lasting implications that it qualifies as an exception to the rule that boards should govern by making policy, rather than by managing the daily work?" If the answer is no, then that particular decision does not belong on the board's agenda.

Instead, the board should ask, "Do we need a policy we don't have, or a change to one we do?" If so, then there might be an appropriate agenda item for the board. If not, the board will do itself a favor by allowing the decisions of its staff to stand.

Four Kinds of Policy

Figure B.1 (see appendix B, page 218) shows a suggested outline for a board policy book. The purpose of a policy book is to keep all of the board's policy decisions easily accessible. Like other board actions, policies are recorded in the minutes when they are adopted, but searching minutes is a tedious and unreliable way to find out what the current policies are. It can also be difficult, until the practice of governing by policy is well established, to know whether a board action taken in response to a particular event was meant to set a precedent or not.

As a first step, it may or may not be a good idea to collect existing policies to plug into the policy book. If you do, you are likely to find that only some of them are truly policies, written to control many decisions over time. Others may turn out, on inspection, to be case law—the board's response to a single event, which then was interpreted as a precedent, whether the board intended it that way or not. One purpose of a policy book is to remove this ambiguity.

After adopting a policy book, the board should from then on clearly identify whether any motion it adopts is meant to be a policy or not. A good rule for a congregation with a policy book is "If it's in the book, it's policy; if it's not in the book, it's not."

The policy book begins with an introductory section that includes a description of the board's philosophy of governance and policies relating to the board's internal processes. This is the place for the board to state the roles of board leaders, its procedure for determining the board agenda, and the charge to board committees. Provisions about individual board members belong here also, including a covenant of expectations and continuing with policies on how the board recruits and trains its members, and procedures for the discipline and removal of board members, should that become necessary.

Four sections follow, one for each of the four zones of congregational decision making: discernment, strategy, management, and oversight (see fig. 5.1, "Roles of Board and Staff," page 91). Appendix B contains suggested and alternative policies organized under the same headings.

Discernment

Discernment includes all that a congregation does to discover and articulate its mission. Typical products of this work include mission and vision statements and a list of core values—all of which should be designed to last for at least several years. The board approves the result of the discernment process, but it cannot and should not do discernment work in isolation. It is appropriate and healthy for the clergy, staff, and program leaders to engage with the board in articulating the purposes for which the congregation exists. But a board that relies on "spiritual experts" to do all of its discernment work abdicates its responsibility. Staff and program leaders have expertise, but the board is the fiduciary, responsible for and to the congregation's mission. A core part of the board's responsibility is to discern and articulate just what that mission is.

At first, board members may feel awkward about discernment. Many boards have little experience of talking about the topics they themselves would say are most important: How do we hope our congregation's ministry with children will transform their lives? What is our mission to the city where we live? What shifts do we see in the religious culture, and how might we need to reframe or adjust our mission statement or our vision in response? Nothing could be more difficult—or more practical—than for a board to spend its time exploring issues like these. Discernment work requires imagination, courage, and tolerance of frank differences—all qualities that are hard to achieve when the board is facing a long list of agenda items! Preferably these kinds of conversations should happen in a spirit of exploration, without the pressure of immediate decisions to be made.

To make time for visionary work, most boards need to create time away from the numbing effects of routine reports and approvals, micromanagement, and problem solving. The most common way to make time is by going on an annual retreat. A better way is to minimize routine items like those described above and explored more fully in chapter 6. With the board agenda cleared, the next challenge is to fill the vacuum. A twelve-month curriculum of visionary conversations is a good way. A board that makes time for visionary work can contribute to the making of the congregation's future in ways only a board can.

Strategy

Deciding when to undertake a capital campaign, setting the overall operating budget, and approving the hiring or dismissal of principal staff members—all these are strategic, "macro-management" decisions, appropriate for the board to make directly if it chooses to. Exactly how detailed the board's strategic policies will be depends partly on its policies on delegation, discussed under "Management," below. Any board should hit the high spots. At any time, a member of the staff or congregation should know (or be able to find out) what major projects the board has chosen for the long and the short term.

The *strategic plan* contains the longest-range plans—though in my experience, few congregations can realistically plan further ahead than five years. A strategic plan answers the question, "What major choices have we made about how we will fulfill our mission?" Because strategic planning happens in the middle section of the map, it involves everyone: congregation, board, and staff. A congregation might form a strategic planning team every five or six years. The team's job is to engage the whole community in "holy conversation" leading to a fresh sense of the congregation's identity, calling, and relationships.[4] The planning team has two primary audiences for its report: if it produces a fresh statement of mission or vision, it is talking mainly to the board. To the extent that it proposes major changes in location, buildings, program emphasis, or staffing, the board is probably its main audience for those recommendations also. If the plan includes timetables, budgets, miscellaneous ideas, and other such specifics, the staff is the principal audience. The planning report should recognize these differences so that it can address the appropriate part of its recommendations to the proper audience.

The *annual vision of ministry* is, as its name suggests, created every year. It answers the question, "In what new and different ways will we transform lives in the next one to three years?" A board retreat is a good context for this work, especially if it can include senior members of the staff and other top ministry leaders. Reflecting on the mission and vision statements, if any, and the strategic plan, if any, the group generates a long list of good ideas and then chooses a short list of priorities. Congregations, at their best, suffer from attention-deficit disorder; two or three priorities are the most they can keep in their collective sights at once.

Another product of the board's annual retreat is a list of *open questions*. In the process of reflecting on its vision of ministry, the board may stumble upon questions that are not ripe to be answered through action or by making them short-term priorities. These questions may relate to major capital projects that cannot happen soon for practical reasons. Or they may arise from changes in the community environment or the surrounding culture that raise doubts as to whether the congregation's comfortable concept of itself is valid anymore. Open questions—sometimes called "frame-bending" or "adaptive" questions—call for a wider, longer conversation than an annual goal-setting process can accommodate. Often the most important open questions facing congregations are versions of the "foundation questions" Gil Rendle and Alice Mann identified in *Holy Conversations*:

- Who are we?
- What has God called us to do and to be?
- Who is our neighbor?[5]

Good open questions are questions that the board truly has no answer for. They become the agenda for "balcony work," when the board, staff, and congregation step aside from the press of daily business and reflect together about how a challenging or changed environment may call the congregation to change in the future.

Boards are often criticized for being secretive or closed. Sometimes they work hard to counter this impression by posting their minutes and announcing in a variety of forums what they have been doing. But the concern behind the criticism is usually not assuaged by such practices. Telling people what you have already decided does not cultivate a sense of openness. Open questions invite conversation before a decision is made. In my experience, nothing prepares a congregation to accept change—even radical change—more effectively than one or several opportunities to talk about the future when the first thing said is, "We will not be making a decision about this soon."

Management

Policies on management serve to delegate parts of the board's power and authority to others. Delegation is essential if the board is to focus on its core roles of discernment, strategy, and oversight. Most practical decisions can safely be made away from the board table, provided that the board adopts clear and limited delegation policies, gives the decision maker guidance as to the larger goals to be achieved, and establishes effective ways to monitor progress and evaluate results. Given such a structure of policy, even boards that otherwise might want to weigh in every month can feel more comfortable delegating more authority and exercising oversight on a less frequent basis.

Some boards are happy to delegate responsibility but stingy about delegating power. If the board wishes to hold others responsible for accomplishing the goals it has adopted, it needs to delegate power and responsibility in matching amounts. The board cannot fulfill its responsibility to the mission on its own, so it must delegate. Delegating a responsibility involves more than simply finding someone who will take it on. The board needs to articulate clearly the larger result it wants, the extent and limits of the power and authority it is prepared to delegate, and a plan for evaluation and accountability. If delegation is to be effective, the board must resist the temptation to review, approve, or second-guess decisions it has delegated. The board can and should evaluate results, but this is better done on schedule, not in response to events. It is never appropriate for a board to delegate authority without articulating the principles by which it wishes that authority to be used. If there are important values to be honored, goals to be achieved, or pitfalls to avoid, the board should say so when it delegates, rather than remembering its principles only at the point of evaluating performance.

Boards more often delegate too little rather than too much. Many boards reserve to themselves all authority to approve special fundraising, to shift money from one budget line to another, or to respond to unexpected needs and opportunities. As important as these decisions are, it is possible to delegate them safely. The key is to articulate a clear vision of ministry, to adopt policies that put boundaries around what can be done, and to establish regular practices of monitoring and evaluation.

Oversight

The board's duty of care requires it to ensure that the congregation's human and material resources are used for the benefit of its mission. The board fulfills this duty both negatively, by preventing theft and loss of resources; and positively, by requiring that the ministry be active, forward-looking, and appropriately bold. To fulfill this responsibility the board needs to say what it wants (through policies on discernment and strategy) and whom it will empower to lead (through policies on delegation). Oversight policies complete this picture by setting standards for the congregation's life and work, and by establishing a plan for monitoring and evaluating that work so that staff and volunteer program leaders are accountable, and so that the congregation learns from its experience.

The standards of care ensure that assets are protected from loss and misappropriation, that people are protected from harm, and that all applicable legal and moral requirements are complied with. For the most part the standards are addressed to the staff, because the staff is responsible for so much of what happens from day to day, but they can be worded broadly, because the same standards for protecting property and people can apply to anyone who leads or manages in the congregation's behalf.

In the area of oversight the buck stops with the board. It can share and delegate pieces of the work—an auditor, for instance, will physically examine the books—but the board is ultimately responsible and cannot shrug off this demand. In some cases individual board members can even be held liable for failure to oversee the institution adequately. Each board member therefore needs at least a basic understanding of the congregation's finances and property, and of the measures taken to ensure that no one who participates in congregational activities is placed at risk.

Often when boards think about their oversight responsibility, they remember their duty to protect the property and manage the money but forget that oversight has a positive aspect as well. Making sure that the congregation acts to fulfill its mission is a part of the board's oversight role. A balanced budget is no virtue if no lives are changed. A budgetary surplus, in this light, may actually reflect a failure of board oversight if it means that people have entrusted it with money that it didn't use for the intended purpose.

Effective oversight requires policies that set up regular routines so that the board can monitor the work and evaluate results.
Monitoring needs to be focused if it is to mean anything: flooding board members with irrelevant paper or tedious oral reports
actually reduces their awareness of how the congregation's ministry is or is not following the guidelines it has laid down or rising
to the goals it has set. In the next chapter we will take a look at
the board's work from a practical standpoint and see how it can
oversee the congregation's work while staying focused on its own
primary work of discernment and strategic thinking.

6 :: Productive Board Meetings

Many board members are dissatisfied with their current way of doing business. They realize they should be "looking at the big picture" or "setting overall direction," but instead they spend much of their time passively listening to reports and talking about pressing but ultimately trivial decisions. Some boards float on clouds of happy talk about how well everything is going; others wallow in a bog of problems and complaints. Boards talk a lot about financial matters, even when some of their members cannot answer basic questions about the congregation's finances. Almost all boards hear too much from a few members and too little from the rest. No wonder so many board members doubt that they are making enough difference to justify their gift of time.

The time involved is not small. The next time you attend a meeting, count the people present. If there are twenty and the meeting runs two hours, it will consume a forty-hour workweek. One response to this alarming fact might be to rush through the meeting, so that it ends sooner. A better response is to put only important work on the agenda and use procedures appropriate to what is to be accomplished. A short, pointless meeting is better than a long one, but a productive meeting trumps them both. If a board is going to use up forty hours of its members' time, it should accomplish a week's worth of good.

This is no small order. To be productive, a board needs to take control of its agenda, so that it can devote its precious time to the best uses. It needs a repertoire of ways to meet, so that it can match the most effective method to a given moment or agenda item. Having learned to do these things, it needs to institutionalize them, so it won't fall back on its old habits.

Taking Control of the Agenda

When I was a parish minister with young children at home, I made it known to all boards and committees that I would be going home at nine o'clock. At the beginning of each meeting, I reminded the group of this, and said, "If there's something on your agenda that you need me to be here for, please put it early." An interesting thing happened: from that day on, almost every meeting ended at nine. The simple act of stopping to think, "What are the most important items on our agenda?" was enough to sharpen the meeting's focus. When it came time to work on unimportant items, they seemed unimportant, so instead we all went home.

My children are grown now, but when I plan a meeting or attend one planned by someone else, I still ask two questions, "When will we go home?" and "What will we accomplish before we go?" Anyone can ask these questions! The best meetings are the ones where someone asks them ahead of time and shapes the agenda around the answers. At the top of a board's agenda, it is a good idea to list one, two, or (at most!) three important things the board will have accomplished by the time it adjourns. The point is not to end on time (though that can be a side effect) but to use time well. The list should name each issue—perhaps as a question—and say what the board will do about it at this meeting. If the intent is to have a good first conversation on an issue, say so. If the board will vote, say that.

For example, an agenda might say that the board intends to address one or two of the following questions:

- What are our ministry priorities for the upcoming two-year period? We will have a first discussion about our priorities, with final approval expected next month, in time to guide the making of a budget.

- How well are we fulfilling our mission with regard to youth? As part of our ongoing process of discernment about the youth, the board will hold a one-hour workshop meeting with the special youth-ministry evaluation committee. Youth representatives will participate. No board action is anticipated.
- Shall we make room for more people by offering worship at one or more additional sites? The board will have a twenty-minute conversation on an idea that might become a goal during the next decade.
- Should we be in the building rental business? Board members will discuss a proposed board policy on rentals. The committee will have modified the proposed policy, basing its action on last month's preliminary conversation. We anticipate a final vote tonight.
- How will the congregation respond to revelations that our bank has practiced racial discrimination in its lending? The board will hear an initial presentation by the treasurer, followed by a conversation focused on such process questions as: How will we gather data? What are our options? Who needs to be involved in this decision? What steps do we need to take before deciding?

By holding up one or two such "big picture" questions as the central themes of a board meeting, an agenda creates a sense of urgency about what could otherwise appear to be routine reports or pro-forma approvals. Appropriate board issues tend to stay around for a long time, so board agendas can be planned months in advance. A yearly routine becomes possible—with predictable recurring events like goal setting, evaluation, and the creation of a budget. Along the way are chances for the board to have deep background discussions of the major points of the congregation's mission, its programmatic and strategic choices, and changes in the community environment. The result may not be shorter meetings, but a well-chosen centerpiece makes the work more likely to be worthy of the time invested. In place of a dull series of small items, each meeting is a feast with a main course.

Governing by Policy

Boards often find it difficult to see how they could shift their agenda to big issues, because their time is already filled up with small ones. Boards often criticize themselves for "micromanaging," and with good reason. Small issues are more interesting and understandable than large ones, and more gratifying to address, because they can be solved more quickly. Oral reports, especially, tempt boards to sidetrack themselves into trivia. Faced with a financial statement, someone wonders, "Why is postage up $650 from last year, when a first-class stamp is still the same?" On hearing a report from the property committee, most boards find it hard to resist latching onto a small but familiar maintenance issue similar to something they have faced at home. Sometimes a board member makes a motion relative to the report (if only to put an end to the conversation), directing the staff or a committee how to do its work. Discussion follows, along with amendments making the directions even more minute. Staff and committee members soon learn to be careful what they tell the board! Boards' fondness for micro-issues is so universal that public-administration theorist C. Northcote Parkinson formulated it into his famous Law of Triviality: "The time spent on any item of the agenda will be in inverse proportion to the sum involved."[1]

Since governing boards have the legal power to control pretty much anything about the congregation's daily business, they are continually tempted to escape from the abstract and sometimes disturbing work of discernment, strategy, and oversight into the micro-world of management decision making. The usual proposed solution is to delegate more management decision making to committees or staff. By itself, this decision rarely solves the problem for long, because it is not only the board but also the larger patterns of the congregational system that cause the difficulty. A board that tries to delegate often finds the matter back on its agenda a month or two later in the form of a progress report or a request to approve an incremental next step. It is not only the board's fascination with concrete decisions that causes it to micromanage but also the timidity of staff and other ministry leaders who may prefer the safety of continually checking back over the rewards and risks of bold decision making.

A strong resolve to avoid micromanagement and to delegate authority is necessary but not adequate to keep a board focused on its real job. To keep from backsliding, the board needs to draw a clear boundary between appropriate and inappropriate board business, empower someone to say no to those who ask to get onto the board's agenda, and then fill up the agenda with equally attractive but appropriate board business; otherwise the little stuff flows in to fill the vacuum. The best way to draw such a boundary is to adopt policies on delegation.

Chapter 5 introduced the policy book as an official repository for board policies. Policies, which control many decisions over time, are a much better way for the board to govern than dealing with individual cases. The rule "If it's a policy, it's in the book; if it's not in the book, it's not policy" is a good way to help a board to take control of its agenda. The transition to governing by policy can feel a bit like trying to get ahead of a runaway wagon in order to start pulling it from the front: until the board has created a more-or-less-complete set of policies, it has to decide cases, because no one else has the authority to decide them. But what is a "more-or-less-complete" set of policies? How should the board create them? How will it know when it has created enough policies that it can safely shift its attention to more appropriate board issues?

John Carver's Mixing Bowls

John Carver, an author and consultant for nonprofit boards, has suggested a helpful analogy for thinking about policy.[2] Policies, he says, are like a set of nested mixing bowls: they come in graduated sizes. The "largest" policies in a given area announce the most general principle or goal the board wishes to achieve. In the area of personal safety, for instance, the largest principle might be that all who participate in congregational activities must be kept safe. A second-level policy might require the staff to follow current best practices for preventing abuse of children and young people who participate in congregational programs. The next-smaller mixing bowl might include several policies that specify some of those best practices: criminal-offender record information (CORI) checks, having two adults present at activities with children or youth, and so on.

Figure 6.1
JOHN CARVER'S MIXING BOWLS

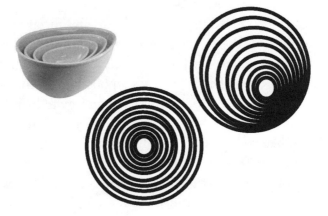

Similarly, in the area of financial management, the top-level policy would say, in effect, "Thou shalt not steal." Midsize policies might require financial managers to be covered by an honesty bond. The most specific policies would say how many signatures a check must have, how cash will be counted, and who can spend budgeted money. A convenient way of representing policies of different sizes is to print them in outline form. The largest policies become the top level of the outline, with related smaller policies below them and indented.

Carver makes the point that if you want to control a set of mixing bowls, you take hold of the outer bowl first, which gives you general control of the whole set. The inner bowls still have limited freedom of movement: they can slosh back and forth a bit within the outer boundary. If you want to control things more closely, you can push your thumbs in toward the center and pin down one or more of the inner bowls. A board can do the same thing with policies, controlling the largest ones directly and leaving the inner ones to the control of others.

An excellent policymaking practice is always to write and adopt policies in order, starting with the largest. After writing each level of policy, the board asks itself, "Have we said enough that we are ready to stop? Are we prepared to accept anything our leaders do so long as it adheres to the policies we have set so far? Or do we want to be more specific?" When boards follow this procedure, they usually stop sooner than they think they will. Stating the board's most general purpose explicitly may seem a bit silly (what board would want to encourage theft?), but it saves a lot of time in the long run, because it provides a secure context for others to fill in the gaps away from the board table.

Policies on Delegation

Making the mixing-bowl approach work begins with writing a strong set of policies that delegate the board's authority to others. The simplest top-level delegation policy empowers the head of staff to make all operational decisions not explicitly reserved to the board, assigned to someone else, or prohibited by other policies. This "global delegation policy" provides a safety net to catch all of the novel items that a congregation tosses up to be decided every day. "How should the thermostats be set?" "Can we take down the lawn sign about last year's humanitarian crisis?" "Can the youth group play the organ?" No board has the foresight and imagination to write policies that anticipate all such questions; what it can do is to invest one person (or a small team) with the power and responsibility to decide them as they come up.

To focus on appropriate board business, the board must set a boundary around its agenda, so that it doesn't end up as the appeals court or *de facto* chief executive. For every decision, someone must be designated as the final decision maker; otherwise, the default decision maker is the board. A board that governs by policy adopts a global delegation policy partly to protect itself from slipping back into micromanagement. Other policies limit the scope of the global delegation policy, give guidance to the ministry decision maker, or delegate specific classes of decisions to someone else.

The four categories of policy discussed in chapter 5 (discernment, strategy, management, and oversight) are the beginning of a road map for a board that wants to create a set of policies. A policy book is "more-or-less complete" when the board has created the entire outer mixing bowl by adopting the largest policies in every category. In chapter 8, we will explore the process by which a congregation might make the transition to governance by policy. Appendix B gives some examples of what the outer ring or two of policies might look like.

Board Committees and Task Forces

A board whose purpose is to "run the church" needs lots of committees to manage programs (sometimes on their own, sometimes in parallel with staff). It also needs committees to help manage ancillary or support functions like finance, building maintenance, and communications.

A board whose purpose is to govern needs fewer committees. The board's function is more focused, and it retains only those committees that relate directly to its primary roles of oversight, strategy, and discernment.

A committee is the creature of its parent, and should do only its parent's work. The test of whether a committee should remain a board committee or become a ministry team is to see where the products of its work go. If a committee takes assignments from the board, and its reports help the board to do appropriate board work, then it is a board committee. If its work produces or supports a program or activity, especially if it works primarily with a staff member, it is better called a ministry team.

The exact list of board committees depends on the exact scope of the board's work as defined by its delegation policies. The board that "runs the church" has delegated nothing—it may give assignments, but it has not delegated true responsibility. Hence its need for an elaborate system of committees. A board that has delegated management to others so that it can govern needs to be careful not to delegate its governance authority as well. The board needs to do its own part of the discernment and strategy work; it cannot give away responsibility for oversight—though it can and should seek help with it. In many cases board committees can and should be temporary—called together when the board needs help with a specific challenge. Standing committees are appropriate only for those areas of policy where the board needs expert counsel regularly.

A minimum list of standing board committees might include finance and personnel committees, both of which help the board create sound policies. Their role stops wherever in the set of mixing bowls the board decides to stop. If they go on to help make further policies—deeper in the set of mixing bowls—they should understand clearly that they have switched bosses, and now work for the leader to whom the board has delegated those small mixing bowls. The personnel committee should not evaluate staff, and the finance committee should not vote to approve spending: those are operational decisions, to be made within the ministry structure, not by board committees. A standing governance committee helps the board to play its own role better (more on this one later in the chapter).

The board can have any number of standing committees to help it do jobs it has decided to control directly. Many nonprofit boards take responsibility for fundraising. There are pros and cons to this practice, but fundraising requires a great deal of detail work best done away from the board table, and a committee is one way to manage this task. A board might have a standing committee to organize and make arrangements for congregational gatherings, including the annual meeting and any town-hall meetings that may take place through the year. Any part of the board's own work is fair game for standing committees.

A second set of board committees might be appointed annually: the audit committee, the nominating committee, and the budget committee (depending on the board's exact role in the budget process—which is a matter of board policy). Annual committees assemble, get their work done, and disband.

Temporary or ad hoc committees—sometimes called task forces—form a third set. The most frequent occasion calling for such a committee comes when the board plans to discuss a critical aspect of the congregation's mission. These committees' job is to prepare for the board to have an excellent conversation on worship, religious education, social outreach, fellowship, new-member ministry, or some other aspect of the congregation's work. Their work might include framing open questions, gathering data, assigning advance homework reading, hiring a facilitator, or setting up the boardroom differently to encourage an informal, workshop-style exchange. It is usually less helpful for committees to frame yes-or-no questions for the board, to present extensive written reports, or to recommend specific outcomes. If a question is appropriate for the board to resolve, it is appropriate for the board to have a rich and nuanced conversation about it. Ad hoc committees that play their role appropriately can make that possible.

The Board Executive Committee

Many boards (or bylaws) empower a small subset of board members to make decisions between meetings. Often the existence of an executive committee is a sign that something needs to be fixed—often a board that is too large. A large board needs an executive to do what the board would do if it were smaller—brainstorm, discern, imagine, and reflect. When the board is very large—twenty-five or more—the executive committee (or some unofficial smaller group) functions as the real board, while the board itself is like a mini-meeting of the congregation. One solution in this case is to expand the executive committee to the perfect size of seven and empower it to do board work, and expand the board to eighty so that it can serve as the larger leadership circle that exists informally in every congregation.

Many executive committees play a special role in personnel decisions, conflicts, and emergencies. While their involvement can be convenient and helpful, it raises the question whether the board could guide the staff leaders sufficiently by policy that it could trust them to make those decisions on their own, consulting with others as they thought prudent. Sometimes executive committees unintentionally stunt the growth of staff decision makers by holding their hands needlessly and providing political cover on issues where the staff should act and accept responsibility.

Some executive committees function as extended gatherings of the senior staff. The presence of several staff members is one clue that this is happening; an agenda full of management decisions is another. This is one way to structure the ministry staff—a topic to which we will return in chapter 7—but it can blur the line between board and staff work, especially if a lay board chair presides. It is one thing to invite a board member to sit in on a staff meeting; framing the staff meeting as a board committee is something else. A board executive committee's work should observe the same boundaries as the board's agenda does.

Probably the most helpful role of an executive committee is to share responsibility with the board chair for stewardship of the board's time. By thoughtfully planning board agendas and coordinating preparation of the meeting packet, an executive committee can strengthen the board without encroaching on the role of staff.

Productive Board Meetings

Once the board gains control of its agenda and sets high expectations for itself, it needs to conduct meetings that produce the results it wants. For many people, *Robert's Rules of Order* is the starting point in thinking about how to run a meeting. This venerable resource is the official parliamentary authority for many congregations and functions unofficially as such in many others. *Robert's* has come in for quite a bit of criticism, some of it justified. Meetings run by *Robert's* can be dull and irritating, with a stereotyped agenda (call to order, reading of the minutes, officer reports, committee reports, old business, new business, adjournment) and much talk of motions and amendments and amendments to amendments. The more mysterious *Robert's* motions—to refer, defer, suspend the rules, adopt the previous question, and place on the table, not to mention arcane interruptions like the point of order, parliamentary inquiry, and question of privilege, are enough to prompt even the most tradition-minded board member to reconsider the whole *Robert's* concept and begin from scratch.

While I understand and sympathize with these frustrations and share many of them, I must rise to defend Brigadier General Henry Martyn Robert, who is less to blame than people think. Quite a bit of the rigidity often ascribed to *Robert's Rules* is nowhere to be found in the book—the 1876 original, the 1915 classic, or the even the endlessly expanded series of "revised" editions.[3] Robert himself is actually pretty flexible: he allows an assembly to adopt its own rules, to proceed as informally as it likes, and to follow any order of business it agrees upon. The original *Robert's* says next to nothing about boards, and the author surely would agree with his revising editors, who say that a small board (twelve or less) may discuss an issue without first putting a motion on the floor; receive a motion without waiting for a second; and talk till everybody has been heard without allowing motions (like the previous question), which, if passed, would squelch debate. The chair of a small board participates in the discussion and votes (unless the bylaws require otherwise) along with everybody else.[4] So far as Robert is concerned, even a large assembly can break into small groups, brainstorm onto newsprint, and burst into song, so long as everyone is given a fair chance to speak to the whole group before it votes.

Poor Robert wrote his rules after trying unsuccessfully to chair a fractious meeting at First Baptist Church, New Bedford, Massachusetts, when he was a young lieutenant recovering from a fever in 1863. The congregation equipped him with "rules" that said vaguely religious things like "love and be kind to one another." Anybody who has poured such balm onto a church fight knows how combustible pious but ambiguous admonishments can be. Wrote Robert: "One can scarcely have had much experience in deliberative meetings of Christians without realizing that the best of men, having wills of their own, are liable to attempt to carry out their own views without paying sufficient respect to the rights of their opponents."[5] Robert had seen meetings railroaded by the determined few, and he wanted rules that would ensure that in the future, each voice would be heard and each vote counted. Robert's purpose, if not every single one of his procedures, should be ours as well. In using *Robert's* with a grain of salt, boards should be careful to preserve the essential rights he wanted to protect:

- the right of the majority to rule,
- the right of individuals to speak and vote, and
- the right of significant minorities to slow the process down so that they can try to persuade others.

Although *Robert's* basic goals are as valid now as ever, his rules fall short of modern boards' requirements. For one thing, they are complex enough that "experts" sometimes use them to accomplish just the sort of railroad job that Robert wanted to prevent. Several simpler parliamentary manuals have tried to correct this problem,[6] but so far, none has achieved wide enough acceptance to succeed as an alternative to *Robert's*. Under any set of parliamentary rules, the chairperson needs to keep things simple and make sure that everyone can follow what is happening.

A second major shortcoming of *Robert's* as a guide to congregational and board decision making is that it works best for "deliberative" meetings, where contending factions argue and the majority decides. But decision is only one useful result that can come out of a meeting. Other outcomes—creative thought and insight, deepened appreciation of personal differences, discernment of God's will—become more likely when meetings are conducted by less formal and contentious methods. Often a creative, "workshop" atmosphere provides a better way to start considering a question, leaving *Robert's Rules* for the decision stage. Workshop facilitation is an art in itself—I will suggest a few of the techniques that have proved most helpful in board meetings.

The Go-around

To establish an egalitarian atmosphere it is essential, early in the meeting, to bring every member fully into the room. A simple way to do this is by having a quick go-around. Ask a question that invites a one-sentence response—for instance, "What did you miss to be here tonight?" "How did this congregation touch your spirit in the past month?" or "Say one word that expresses part of how you're feeling as we start our meeting." The go-around accomplishes at least two things: It gives an opportunity for anyone who may be bursting with some bad (or good) news to get it out before it interferes with his or her participation. The go-around allows such news to surface early and gives others a chance to respond supportively.

A second major benefit of the go-around stems from a fact of group psychology: If everybody speaks at the beginning of a meeting, even if some of them say, "I pass," the group will share airtime more equitably from then on. The go-around helps avoid one of the most time-wasting patterns boards experience, which is that the views of certain board members are not made part of the conversation soon enough. Sometimes the first sign of dissent comes when a member votes against, or abstains from voting on, a motion that appeared until that moment to have had unanimous support. While it may seem efficient to move on, taking silence for assent, assent is not necessarily what silence means. After the meeting, members who, for whatever reason, held their peace may subtly or not so subtly undermine the board's decision. A go-around can be a helpful way to encourage board members to fulfill their duty of care by taking part in board discussion, and their duty of loyalty by expressing their dissent at meetings of the board, not afterward.

The go-around is not a bad idea now and then throughout a meeting. For all their seeming rationality, boards are emotional systems composed of people who, at any moment, carry feelings, preoccupations, prejudices, and attitudes that control the meeting whether they are recognized or not. The go-around honors the complexity of a roomful of human beings and helps them to become a board more capable of thinking, feeling, choosing, and discerning as a group.

Acting Small

From the point of view of group process, the ideal board has seven members. A group that size finds it relatively easy to retain control of its agenda and to keep each member feeling responsible for the board's work. From the point of view of democracy, a seven-member board has some surprising advantages. Unlike a larger board, it can be under no illusion that its members fully "represent" the congregation. Small boards know that if they want congregational support (and they need it, whether they want it or not!), they have to engage constituents in continual two-way communication through committees, surveys, town meetings, and informal one-to-one exchange. A large board has all it can do to achieve a quorum and bring board members up to speed, so that they can discuss and vote. Having done that work, the board may feel democratic, even though the entire process has been internal to the board. A small board is continually reminded—simply by looking around the table—that it is too small to represent the congregation without communicating with the other members actively.

Reducing the board to seven members often is not politically realistic, especially in congregations with fewer than about 250 active members. (Larger congregations, interestingly enough, see the value of a smaller board more easily.) For many boards, the challenge is to function well despite being bigger than might be ideal.

Suppose, for instance, that a board of twenty-five has an important decision to make. If a group that large begins, in standard *Robert's Rules* style, with a motion and debate, it typically will hear at length from two or three members who are (1) comfortable speaking to a group of twenty-five, and (2) already have opinions. If the motion was presented as the report of a committee, the debate may take the form of a series of questions or criticisms addressed to the committee representative, who may speak several times, explaining or defending the report. After the most opinionated members have spoken, a strong impression will have been created that one side or the other has the advantage—or that the board is evenly divided. At that point, someone "calls the question"[7] and a vote is put. Often the decisive argument is that the board should respect (that is, approve) the work of its committee, which might make you wonder why the congregation needs a board; or that the majority of the board should rule, which might make you wonder why it needed a committee. Whatever the outcome, a large board that follows a formal, large-group debate model stacks the odds against real interchange or increased understanding.

One method for achieving some of the advantages of a small board is to break a big one into groups after a motion is made or a question has been posed. The chairperson may hand over leadership to someone else, either to make use of special workshop-facilitation skills or simply to punctuate the transition to a different kind of meeting. The facilitator asks the board to form for a few minutes into groups of two, three, four, or five. The first instruction to the small groups might be, "Please come up with three questions about the report we have just heard," or "State three religious values that inform your reflections on this issue," or "Think of a Bible story about a time God's people faced a situation similar in some way to this one." After five or ten minutes (the facilitator should announce the time frame in advance, and warn the groups when time is nearly up), ask one group to give *one* of its responses to the question. Rather than walking through a full report from each small group (a procedure likely to be so slow and repetitive that the board will never want to hear "small groups" again), the facilitator then can repeat the first response and say, "Who else said something similar?" When the variations on the first theme are exhausted, the chair repeats the process—possibly with someone listing major themes (not individual responses) on newsprint or a whiteboard.

At this point, the board can return to formal business mode, knowing that each member, having spoken at least once in the small group, will be more likely to speak to the full board and that the full range of opinion has been laid out on the board table.

The large group will still be a large group, but a brief detour into small-group mode will have improved its capacity to speak and listen.

Pre-processing Decisions

Here's a political tip: the most important virtue any proposal can have going for it is that members of the board have heard of it before. People are naturally uncomfortable with change, and so the first time any idea comes up before a board—no matter how familiar it may be to those who propose it—for most people it is easier to find objections than to see advantages. This principle applies to committees, ministry teams, and congregational meetings: if a vote on a proposed change is taken the same day people hear about it for the first time, the chances are against it. So if you want your idea to pass, it is not a good idea to begin by arguing for it. Arguing (however civilized and pleasant) only activates people's rational capacities, which they employ to argue back. The most successful first campaign for a new idea is a "mentioning" campaign. Mention that you've heard about a new idea that some other congregation (perhaps in California, if you're not in California) has tried. The next week, mention that you heard that a couple of congregations were trying the same thing in Kansas (unless you are in Kansas). The third week, simply raise the general issue. Someone will say, "Don't you know? Here's what all the other congregations do."

The same principle is helpful even if, instead of wanting to persuade board members of a particular idea, you simply want them to have a good, open-minded conversation. You know that familiar ideas tend to crowd out new ones, and you want to shuffle a fair deck for a decision your board needs to make soon. In that case, it is a good idea to have one or more meetings where the first thing said is, "We will not make a decision about this today." Set a time limit, provide a manageable amount of information, and let the conversation flow. When time is up, say, "As planned, we have not arrived at a conclusion. We can declare this part of the agenda a success! We will return to this topic next month, with the benefit of the head start we gave ourselves today."

The pre-meeting meeting is just as valuable, if not more so, for the congregation as a whole or for the top eighty to 120 leaders. (Interestingly enough, this seems to be about how many people seriously expect to influence decisions in congregations from eighty to ten thousand members.) The most important thing when seeking input from the board's constituents is to be sure to do it soon enough. A meeting to "discuss the board's recommendation" is much less attractive than "a meeting to help the board to decide what to recommend." If you want to keep the board (or congregation) focused on the big picture, a good way to do so is to plan some meetings where the first thing said is, "We will not make a decision about this today."

Consent Agenda

A helpful way of keeping a board out of the "micro–mind-set" is to divide its agenda into two parts: a consent agenda and a discussion agenda. The consent agenda, which contains actions the board will take without discussion, has become a widely recognized best practice for nonprofit boards.[8] Its purpose is to deal quickly with the necessary but essentially routine things a board must act on, so that the board can spend its time on its main work of discernment, strategy, and oversight.

What sort of business belongs on a consent agenda? Approval of the minutes, certainly. Most reports belong in the board packet, and most of the requests that reports contain belong there, too. The consent agenda might include items to approve signing a contract for a project the board has already approved, to shift money from one budget to another, to empower the treasurer to open a new bank account, to adjust deductibles on an insurance policy, to update personnel policies to conform to new laws, to accept people into membership, or to certify the congregation's delegates to regional or national meetings. Some of these matters may, of course, be delegated, in which case the board need not vote on them at all. But sometimes a board needs to vote directly on them, because the bylaws say so, or because the board has chosen to reserve the final decision to itself. The consent agenda makes it possible for the board to use its authority without needing to spend time chatting about matters whose outcome is not in serious question.

At the board meeting, the board chair says at the commencement of the business portion of the meeting, "You have all received the board packet with the consent agenda. Does any member wish to move an item from the consent agenda to the discussion agenda?" If any member requests it, an item is moved. (By courtesy, advance notice would be given to the board chair.) The chair then says, "Without discussion, we are ready for a vote on the consent agenda. Those in favor? Opposed? All items on the consent agenda are adopted."

Note that there is *never* a discussion about the consent agenda, or about whether an item does or does not belong there. Individual board members read the board packet and come prepared to move items to the discussion agenda—or forever hold their peace.

The consent agenda requires a disciplined approach to preparing the board packet. The person or team responsible for creating the agenda also is responsible for the board packet, for seeing that it gets to every board member in a timely way, and for deciding what to include in the consent agenda. An example of a consent agenda policy is in appendix B. *All* reports should be *received* through the consent agenda. (Reports should hardly ever be "approved" in any case—that would mean the board agreed with every word.) The only reason a report might be presented orally during the board meeting would be to set the table for a main-course conversation. Different people absorb information differently—and a brief oral report can reinforce, for auditory learners, something that visual learners have already gotten from the packet. The oral report brings everyone to equal readiness so that the board can have a better discussion. That is quite different from a report that takes board time simply to advance the general goal of "knowing what is going on."

After adopting the consent agenda, the board moves on to the discussion agenda, which ideally contains only two or three items, plus any consent items that have been moved to it. The result is that the board spends more time addressing topics it has identified in advance as important, less time responding to particular issues that have arisen, and no time listening passively to reports.

A Regular No-Staff Huddle

Here's an idea that makes clergy hair stand up whenever I suggest it: every month hold a brief board session without clergy or staff members present. This notion seems strange to many people, but it has become an accepted practice in the corporate world, where too many boards are passive rubber stamps for management. The Sarbanes-Oxley Act of 2002—a federal law enacted in response to scandals at Enron, WorldCom, and other corporations—recognizes the important difference between board members who are and are not on the company payroll. Sarbanes-Oxley gives "independent" board members of publicly traded corporations a special role as guardians of governance, critics of management strategy, and objective arbiters of CEO compensation. Rules adopted by the stock exchanges under Sarbanes-Oxley require that outside board members be a majority of the board and that they meet regularly by themselves.[9] The logic is clear: If non-employee board members are to play a special role, they need to meet alone from time to time.

Most of Sarbanes-Oxley does not apply to nonprofits or congregations directly,[10] but the logic behind regular meetings of board members who are not also employees—if it becomes a lasting part of business culture—is likely to find its way into the congregational boardroom. Already in the secular nonprofit world, a regular short gathering of independent board members at the end of each board meeting has become a widely recommended practice.[11] All volunteer board members have a brief conversation about how the meeting went and raise any concerns. Right after the board adjourns, the chair or other designated leader briefs the head of staff about any concerns or issues raised during the board huddle, especially anything touching on the board's relationship with the staff.

While the board huddle technically is a type of executive session, the term is misleading. For one thing, the "executives" have left the room. Also, "executive session" usually means a meeting held to deal with sensitive or confidential matters, from which the board may (or must) exclude those who should not be involved in order to protect confidentiality or other important interests. Executive sessions may, and often do, include appropriate staff members.

The board huddle is different. The staff is not ejected, but leaves by mutual agreement, so volunteer board members have a time to meet separately, as the staff does. Like any other executive session, the board huddle has a defined agenda, and it is not appropriate to stray into other matters or to take action while the staff members are absent. The agenda for the board huddle is board self-management: How are we doing as a board? Are there interpersonal tensions among board members that are getting in the way? What went especially well? What would we do differently if we could? Are there topics we need to raise with the clergy leader? Other items may be added to the board huddle agenda, preferably in consultation with the clergy leader, but the chair should make sure the huddle does not degenerate into gossip or backbiting. The minutes show a summary of topics raised, and the chair briefs the clergy leader as soon as possible. If other staff members were discussed, they are briefed as well. If potential conflicts surface, they are noted and identified, to be addressed with all parties present.

By meeting regularly without the staff and clergy, the board takes away some of the drama that so often attaches to executive sessions. When held only in times of staff-related conflict, an executive session will itself ratchet up the sense of crisis. A great deal depends, of course, on lay board members' willingness to apply good judgment during their time alone. Of course, *not* holding an executive session is no guarantee that members will use good judgment in the parking lot!

The lay-only huddle is a new idea and not well tested yet, but early feedback from boards that have tried it suggests it can improve the sense of board-staff partnership by giving lay board members a chance to see and feel themselves as a distinct group with distinct responsibilities.

Institutionalizing Good Board Practice

A board that institutes even a fraction of the advice given above will find its work considerably changed. But human systems tend strongly to return to old familiar ways, especially under stress. To institutionalize effective meeting practices, board members need to formalize their expectations of each other and to assign responsibility for keeping watch, so the board can shore up its best practices and keep them fresh.

Creating a Board Covenant

Today, even more than in Robert's time, it is a mistake to assume that everyone who sits at a board table brings the same expectations about behavior, decision making, problem solving, or courtesy. Assumptions differ so sharply that each board needs to develop its own covenant of shared behavioral expectations and review it regularly. New members of the board need to be brought into the covenant and invited to help reshape it. A helpful resource for creating such covenants in groups of any size is *Behavioral Covenants in Congregations: A Handbook for Honoring Differences* by Gil Rendle.

Boards can be surprisingly resistant to firm expectations. Some members seem almost to prefer complaining about others to stating clearly what the board expects. Sometimes people say, "We have enough trouble getting people to agree to serve without making this even more difficult." This concern sounds reasonable, but experience shows that people are more attracted to highly disciplined groups than to lax ones. This is especially true of people who can make the greatest contribution. The board member who likes to cruise into every other meeting unprepared may enjoy that freedom, but he or she makes the board experience much more frustrating for everyone else. Expectations can be firm and clear without needing to be rigid or unreasonable.

Basic duties. In creating a board covenant, a good place to begin is with a frank discussion about the basic duties of board membership: attendance at meetings, diligent preparation, and thorough understanding of the congregation's overall situation. Some members may have accepted nomination despite known schedule conflicts. These need to be resolved or explicitly excused, or else those members need to leave the board if it is to arrive at manageable baseline expectations.

Some boards have an automatic resignation policy, either in the bylaws or in their covenants. If a board member misses more than a set number of meetings, he or she is deemed to have resigned and is so notified. Other boards give warning notices and phone calls before asking members to come back or please resign—but why? How does treating people like children help them to be more responsible? It is reasonable to expect adults to understand the consequences of their own decisions, especially if they have agreed to them.

Nothing helps people to arrive on time more than starting whether they have arrived or not. Likewise, the best way to encourage members to read the packet is to assume that everyone has read it, and proceed. Of course, the packet needs to be of reasonable length and focused on important issues, and it must be published to board members in a timely way. E-mail fortunately makes the packet easy to publish, but unfortunately also makes it easy to be careless about dumping reams of reading onto a board without vetting it for relevance. The board's covenants about its work routines need to include limits on how much the board expects of members.

Shared study and spiritual practice. In working with boards to create covenants, I urge them to explore topics that make them uncomfortable. Often one such topic is the board's spiritual practice. In many churches, board members expect the spiritual life of the board to start and end with a prayer by the pastor. Group prayer is fine, but I know of no tradition that requires prayer to be led by an ordained leader. I would encourage any board to give its clergy a year's vacation from praying at board meetings, so lay members can take turns doing it themselves. Synagogue boards commonly hear a *d'var Torah* (literally "a word of Torah") from the rabbi at the beginning of board meetings, a practice I would recommend to anyone. The rabbi comments briefly on a Torah text, connecting it to something about the organizational life of the synagogue or even something on the board's agenda—preferably without taking sides. Here, too, I would encourage sharing the practice with lay board members. Taking turns would be one way, though it can also be fruitful to take a few minutes to study a text in small groups, reflecting on a question posed by the leader.

One useful format for group reflection on a text is sometimes called African (or Lambeth) Bible study. A text is read several times, possibly by different readers, perhaps in different translations. After each reading, members respond to a simple question ("What one word or image stays with you from this passage?"

"How does this passage touch you personally?" "How might this passage inform our work this evening?"). A small board can go around the table hearing a response from every member; if the group is larger, it can break into subgroups of three to five. With a leader who can keep the group on task, even a full three-reading study can occur in fifteen or twenty minutes—too much for every month, perhaps, but not too much to spend on bringing the stories of the larger faith community to bear on the board's work once in a while.

Some boards' study covenants ask every member to do ongoing homework. This assignment may mean reading a chapter of a book each month and taking a few minutes to discuss it at a meeting. The book might be of a religious nature, or it might address an organizational or moral issue. Choosing common readings is a privilege the board should delegate with care, so that the readings challenge the board while giving no one reason to feel excluded because of having had an education different from that of other members of the board.

It is not important that a board adopt any specific spiritual or study practice. It is important that it be in conversation periodically about what practices it deems appropriate, and that it ask each member to commit to a shared routine that touches the transcendent meanings of the board's work. The benefits are difficult to predict precisely, but boards that engage regularly in spiritual practice grow in their ability to speak frankly in love and to stay focused on the congregation's mission.

Financial support. Even more challenging, on many boards, than covenanting to engage in spiritual practice is defining expectations about members' financial support of the congregation. Many nonprofit boards espouse the Three G Rule: "Give, Get, or Get Off." Board members are expected to contribute generously and to acquire large gifts from others—or to resign. To many congregations this rule may seem too harsh. Including people in diverse economic circumstances in the congregation and its leadership may be a core value.

Because they care about inclusiveness (and because they dislike confrontation), boards often err in the opposite direction and say nothing at all about what they expect board members to contribute. This omission can lead to the bizarre but not uncommon result that a board in whose name the congregation asks for generous support includes a member who can afford as much as others can, but who gives little or nothing. By the power of negative example, this kind of behavior by leaders has its effect on the congregation's overall giving even if it is, in theory, secret.

It is tricky but possible to define expectations for board members' giving that are both clear and inclusive. Simply to announce the total giving by board members to the board itself can make a difference. Paying attention to this total gives the message that board members' giving is important. In addition, it can be helpful for the board to set a goal for its own giving from year to year.

Another approach is to define an overall standard (a percentage of income or even a dollar amount) and then acknowledge that no one standard will be reasonable for everyone, so some generous members will give less, but fortunately others can and will give more. One way of stating the expectation is to say that each board member is expected to consider giving at the requested standard, and will have a conversation with one other board member about how he or she arrived at a decision.

There will always be board members who, for various reasons, cannot give as much as others do. Rather than letting this limitation inhibit those who can give more from celebrating and encouraging each other, it is best for the board covenant to articulate an expectation that board members will be generous in support of the congregation and mindful that their example influences the congregation as a whole.

Decision making and conflict management. A final topic a board covenant needs to address is how the board will make decisions and manage conflict. These topics go together: decision making is difficult only when people disagree. Some boards assume that voting is an adequate system for resolving conflicts, but it's not. Voting may be a fairer way to make decisions than arm-wrestling, but it is no less an exercise in power. The majority has the legal right to compel the congregation to accept its views. By prevailing in a vote, the majority tacitly invokes the power of the state—the courts and even the police—to enforce its will. Surely, this is not ideal from a religious point of view!

It may surprise some people to know that General Robert was a great believer in consensus. In his own civic work, he went to great lengths to avoid divided votes, which he regarded, especially in a small board, as a mark of failure. Many arcane motions—to commit, refer, postpone, and place before a committee of the whole—essentially are ways to buy time for more discussion as an alternative to rushing to a vote. Robert gave what he called "substantial minorities"—more than one-third—the right to stop the majority from barging ahead and to require a slower, more deliberate process. Robert also understood that *requiring* unanimity can lead to tyranny by the minority. It is as unfair for the few to prevent the many from deciding as it would be for the many to prevent the few from trying to change the majority's minds.

A covenant might well provide a process to identify decisions that need special attention and would benefit from a more gradual process of discernment. Such decisions merit one or more "pre-meeting meetings"—meetings with "a discussion that is only a discussion." Such meetings lower the temperature considerably and increase the chance of finding a compromise or a third way that will allow the group to stand united in the end. A board might also covenant to seek assistance from the denomination or an outside facilitator if conflict overwhelms the board's ability to deal with it alone.

The Governance Committee

Techniques alone—including those discussed here—cannot sustain a productive board by themselves. Consistent high performance requires structures that make it someone's job to monitor the board's performance and engage it in continual improvement. The board governance committee is one such structure. An integral part of the board, this committee is responsible for helping the full board to live up to its role in governance, its meeting practice, and its covenant of expectations. The governance committee maintains a job description for board members and a list of skills and qualities the board needs. It works with (or even replaces) the nominating committee in recruiting new board members, balancing representative democracy with a conviction that the congregation deserves the best board it can obtain. Since board effectiveness is one of the things most congregations want, there need be no conflict between democracy and excellence.

The exact duties of a governance committee depend on the specifics of the role and process the board chooses for itself. The governance committee leads an annual training session for new board members, to which "old" board members are invited, and facilitates an annual review of the board covenant. It may have other duties—for example, to help with the board's annual self-evaluation. Some board governance committees recruit a talent pool of people with gifts in meeting facilitation, on whom the board chair can call in moments that require a process that looks more like a workshop than a deliberative assembly. The governance committee's job, in short, is to enable the board to become the best and most productive board it can.

7 :: Lay and Clergy Partnership

The relationship of lay and clergy leaders has a colorful American history. From the earliest struggles between ministers and magistrates in Puritan New England to recent headlines about abusive clergy and their stunned parishioners, high drama has rarely ceased. Clergy and their lay employers—or to put it differently, lay members and their clergy leaders—experience highs and lows found only among people who care deeply about the purposes for which they partner.

American congregations have rarely tolerated clergy leadership without resisting it. For the first Europeans in most parts of colonial North America, clergy power was not a worry; lay settlers came first and set up congregations on their own. For lay leaders throughout the colonies, the hazard of excessive clergy power was a continual concern. For clergy, the burden of *lay* power was a daily fact of life. Even in New England, contrary to the stereotype of the tyrannical Puritan "theocracy," struggles to contain the power of clergy began in the 1600s and have never stopped. From earliest days, American clergy have complained of being hemmed in, censored, and kept poor by wary laity—not everywhere and always, but often enough to have produced an occupational resentment still expressed wherever clergy gather.

Many lay and clergy leaders work together happily, disagree without explosion, and feel strong in their roles without needing to diminish one another. Almost any organizational structure you can imagine works well in a congregation somewhere, thanks to the social skills and dedication of its leaders. Such exceptions are no proof that structure doesn't matter. Structure and other formal understandings matter most when social skills are less than perfect and when dedication comes mixed with ordinary human traits like selfishness, ambition, vanity, and pride—that is, all the time. Some clergy seem to have consistent positive relationships wherever they go; some congregations seem to have consistent positive relationships as clergy come and go. If we are interested in positive relationships, we would do well to pay attention to the practices such clergy and congregations follow.

One such practice is to showcase the good relationship of the most visible lay and clergy leaders. President and rabbi, council chair and pastor, clerk of session and minister—these leaders, under any titles, symbolize for the congregation the tone of the whole leadership. If possible, they should appear before the congregation regularly, to affirm the importance of one another's role, teach about differences and boundaries, and visibly enjoy their jobs. If their actual relationship is so bad that they can't do this, they should make extraordinary efforts to improve it; if they still can't, one of them needs to resign. If they can't choose which, the board should do it for them. It makes no sense at all for a congregation to pay good money (or even mediocre money) for the privilege of watching leaders gradually whittle one another down to nothing. Harmonious top lay and clergy leaders can be an invaluable influence on other leaders and the congregation as a whole.

Lay leadership is not the same as governance, and clergy leadership is not the same as ministry. Governing boards in most traditions include clergy, who have considerable influence even when they do not vote. Ministry, as we are using the word, includes all the daily, practical work of the congregation, no matter who does it. Still, tension between laity and clergy often spills over into the relationship of board and staff and fosters many of the mistakes congregations make in structuring themselves.

For instance, in the committee-centered model described in chapter 3, congregations set up a double power structure—

committees on one side, staff on the other—in joint charge of the same subject matter, often without placing a clear boundary between their spheres of responsibility. Sometimes the rationale for this arrangement is frankly to provide "checks and balances"— committees watch out to make sure staff (and especially clergy) doesn't have too much power. The committee-centered structure frequently succeeds at keeping anyone from having too much— or even barely enough—power. With ministry and governance fused from knee to shoulder, no one quite defines the mission; no one quite carries it out. With authority shared so completely, no one can be held accountable. Out of its anxiety about excessive clergy power, the congregation reduces its own power to do what it is meant to do. The idea of checks and balances—a venerable and valid principle of governance—needs to be incorporated in a structure that leaves space for independent action and initiative, a fruitful partnership of lay and clergy leaders.

Firm Boundaries

What does a fruitful partnership require? Many people say collaboration is the key—which is, it seems to me, 100 percent half right. Open, relaxed, flexible relationships, lubricated by some social time, are indispensable to board-staff partnership. But openness is not all; partnership also requires firm boundaries—clarity about what decisions the board makes and which it delegates; clarity about who leads the staff, and what authority belongs to that role; clarity, for every category of decisions, about who leads the process, who is consulted, who finally decides, and who picks up the ball after the decision and takes charge of getting the work done. Firm boundaries do not mean stilted relationships. When it is clear where each buck will stop and who will bear each cross, daily interactions between board, clergy, and staff can actually be more relaxed and flexible than when roles need to be renegotiated every day. Firm boundaries fall at the center of a spectrum, with rigid boundaries at one end, fuzzy boundaries at the other.

Rigid board-staff boundaries are marked by secrecy and exclusion; fuzzy ones by frequent, anxious checking in and checking on and checking back. Rigid boundaries are brittle and prone to conflict; fuzzy ones are confusing and prone to painful misunderstandings. Firm boundaries are just right. They require clear guidance by the board, willing accountability by staff, and unshakable respect by each for the other's sphere.

Boundaries for the board-staff partnership are defined to some extent by bylaws and such documents. The board delineates them further by adopting delegation policies. For many boards, policies about the structure and authority of staff are challenging to write. What is the best or most appropriate staff structure for a congregation of our size? How much of what kind of power should the board delegate? How should we integrate paid staff with the volunteers who also act as leaders and workers in the area of ministry? What process of goal setting and evaluation will promote high staff morale and creativity while achieving the board's goals and ensuring that its policies are honored? No one answer to these questions fits all congregations, but certain benchmarks are worth considering by any board as it makes choices about staff authority and structure. Effective delegation policies will

- Minimize the number of individuals and groups that report directly to the board, so that the board can concentrate on discernment, strategy, and oversight.
- Match delegated responsibility with delegated power, so that staff can reasonably be held accountable for outcomes.
- Encourage staff to form a strong and self-sufficient team whose members take individual and joint responsibility, manage their own relationships, and resolve their own differences.
- Create a single structure for decision making about ministry. Encourage wide consultation, but avoid triangulation by placing the final decision for each class of decisions in one place.

- Ensure that the staff's structure and style of operation honor and express the congregation's values. For a faith community, the way the work is done is as important as the measurable outcomes.

With attention to these goals, a board can create delegation policies that encourage the firm, just right boundaries that give even less-than-perfect leaders a good chance at creating and sustaining fruitful partnership.

Delegating Power and Authority

Firm boundaries require the board to delegate authority. Delegation policies grant to the staff (and possibly to others) power to make decisions so that the board won't need to. Having delegated a decision, the board needs to hold its side of the boundary and refuse to jump in and try to fix things.

Delegating authority is not the same as assigning a task. An assignment is a one-time thing; delegation covers a whole class of matters and entrusts the delegate to exercise discretion in unforeseen situations. The board can and should give guidance when it delegates, and evaluate performance and results after the fact. But if it parcels out its guidance all along the way, its delegation is undone.

A board that fails to delegate—and to delegate generously—diminishes its own authority, because it neglects its larger work while trying to pull every string. Which is more important, after all—the power to vote on every cent spent out of the congregation's coffers, as my great-grandfather's session did, or the authority to interpret mission and choose strategies? The answer may seem obvious, but in an anxious congregation with a history of turf struggles, it can be difficult for boards to trust that they can give away authority without losing it for good.

One key to a successful board-staff partnership is to understand that power is not a fixed commodity. Practices that treat power as a finite resource are self-confirming: by hampering the institution as a whole, they create a false impression of scarcity and foster competition for what little power remains. The power to *compel* others does come in fixed amounts—measured, often, in dollars. But the power of a board that uses its purse-strings power to compel obedience, like the power of a clergy leader who "controls" the board, is largely an illusion. Compulsion is at best a zero-sum game, because 99 percent of any congregation's power is persuasive, not compulsive. The power of influence, persuasion, and example is expandable—not infinitely, but in most faith communities, well beyond current limits. The power of a congregation whose board governs strongly and empowers staff to act strongly is limited mainly by the daring of the vision the members create together.

Structuring the Staff

Making the clergy leader head of staff is the simplest and most common way to structure staff authority. There are other ways, but the more variety I see, the more partial I become to the simplicity of one head of staff. The board's global delegation policy (discussed in "Policies on Delegation," chapter 6) empowers the head of staff to make any decision not otherwise addressed by policy. When the board speaks to the staff, it speaks to the head of staff, who represents the whole ministry structure to the board. (Other staff or lay leaders will sometimes do the actual talking, but the head takes responsibility for what they say.) A great advantage of this straightforward system is that the board has only one person reporting to it directly, a practice that minimizes the time the board spends directing, guiding, and evaluating staff members, and mediating differences among them.

Being head of staff fits some aspects of the clergy role better than others. It fits the fact that symbolically the clergy leader is the head of the congregation—regardless of what the bylaws say— and is seen as such by many members and all passersby. Even in congregations where clergy have little power to make decisions, their symbolic role gives them moral authority. In the long run, what the clergy leader pays attention to will grow; what he or she ignores will shrink. Moral authority is persuasive—influence without compulsion—but effective. A congregation depends so much on volunteers that moral authority alone can mobilize a significant portion of its resources. To make those resources productive, though, the clergy leader needs things only the board can grant. Money, building space, staff time—without these, the rights and privileges of ordination mean very little. Without the board's support—or at least its tacit sufferance—visible signs of ministry grind to a halt. The clergy leader as the symbolic head of the congregation and the board as holder of its material resources are natural and necessary partners in the congregation's leadership.

Like many other managers today, a clergy leader is first not a manager at all, but a member of a profession—a priest, pastor, minister, or rabbi. He or she may lack specific managerial skills like supervision, budgeting, and project planning. Board members, who may be expert managers themselves in other industries, may judge the clergy leader unqualified to head the staff. Most congregations say on surveys that they want clergy to spend time in worship preparation, study, writing, pastoral care—almost anything except "administration." The clergy leader may agree, and happily avoid responsibility for management—at least in theory. In practice, most congregations expect clergy to play a larger management role than they realize. Management decisions must be made, and the person on the scene best suited to make them, often, is the clergy leader. The larger and more complex the congregation, the more time and energy administration takes. Clergy find themselves in the uncomfortable position of controlling and feeling responsible for operations without formal authority to do so. What is the solution?

Clergy and congregations are not alone in this dilemma. Top leaders of many modern institutions have primary expertise in a profession rather than in management per se. Hospital CEOs are often doctors, college presidents are usually scholars, and museum directors often begin as artists or art historians rather than as managers. Business leaders, too, increasingly think of themselves as engineers, economists, or marketers who happen to be working as managers. I once heard Dr. Roy W. Menninger, a psychiatrist who succeeded his father and uncle as head of the Menninger Clinic, say that at first he treated the clinic and its managers as if they were patients. When his department heads came to him with management issues, he gave them sympathy, analysis, support, and understanding, but they seemed dissatisfied. Later, he became a more effective leader when he realized that in his administrative role people didn't come to him for healing; they came wanting him to make decisions.

Professionals can make good staff leaders because they understand and care about the core work of the institution, be it medicine, education, art, technology, engineering, finance, or the building of a community of faith. But leadership alone is not enough. Organizations also need someone to make decisions and coordinate the work. Clergy who become institutional leaders need to learn some managerial skills like project and financial management and supervision. They need to develop managerial traits like decisiveness, clear boundaries, and a willingness to disappoint people. They also need to cultivate their sense of calling. Other staff can complement a clergy leader's deficits in managerial skill, but it's hard to work around a leader who has lost the heart to lead.

Talking with clergy, I sometimes suggest that management, according to a common definition, means "getting results through the efforts of others." Thinking about it that way, some clergy (and board members, too) see that a clergyperson may bring more strengths to staff leadership than they first thought, and that his or her deficits may not be so serious, given the availability of "others" who know things the staff leader does not. The challenge, especially for clergy who have moved from smaller congregations to larger ones (or who have found themselves in larger congregations without moving) is to cultivate a style of management that feels like ministry. The board can support this transition by selecting a staff structure that enables the staff leader to achieve religiously appropriate results with the support of others who contribute needed managerial skills.[1]

An effective plan for congregations with 150 to 400 active members is to make the clergy leader head of staff and to hire an administrator to take charge of building maintenance, budgeting, and finance. All building and administrative staff (custodians, secretaries, bookkeepers) report to the administrator. The administrator reports to the clergy leader along with senior program staff—music and education directors, volunteer coordinator, and so on. The administrator manages the technical/managerial aspects of the staff's work, including, for example, staff goal setting and evaluation, staff policies on building use, and fiscal matters. The staff team integrates business and program dimensions into a unified set of plans and goals, under the leadership of a pro in the congregation's primary line of work.

The Executive Number Two

In congregations big enough to support a second staff member with both program and administrative skills, a common model is to have only one staff member report directly to the senior clergy leader: an executive number two. This structure allows the clergy leader to focus on such things as visionary leadership, fundraising, and high public visibility. The number two—under the title executive minister, church administrator, or temple director—supervises other staff, convenes staff meetings, coordinates reporting to the board, and takes responsibility for ministry performance overall. The number two position requires strong management skills, a strong understanding of the congregation's religious mission, and a relationship of total trust with the clergy leader. In business, analogous roles are often designated chief executive and chief operating officer. In colleges and universities, the president and provost often have a similar relationship, as do the president and executive director of some secular nonprofits. In the U.S. Navy, a ship's master (captain) decides strategy and relates to the larger command structure, while the executive officer (XO) runs the ship.

One search committee, looking for a number two, described the hoped-for applicant this way: "If you are a minister, people say to you, 'You could have been in business.' If you're a businessperson, people say, 'You should have gone to seminary.'" They found their candidate—a master of divinity who had an M.B.A. as well.

The number-two arrangement appeals to many boards because of a special aspect of the clergy leader's role. More than most nonprofit leaders, clergy leaders are accountable to bodies other than the board. The congregation, the denomination, the seminary or rabbinical school—each owns a piece, making the relationship of a clergy leader with the board more complex than that of an executive director to the board in most nonprofits. The exact nature of the special clerical authority varies by tradition; it may include the right to make decisions about worship and ritual, and freedom to speak from personal conviction in the sanctuary and elsewhere. The number two—even when he or she reports to the senior clergy leader—can be accountable to the board for staff performance in a simpler, less divided way.

Collective Leadership

Congregations have tried a number of alternatives to the clergy-head-of-staff structure, with varying success. Probably the most common is to vest management decision making in the board executive committee. This arrangement tends to blur the boundary between board and staff. The more involved in staff decision making leaders of the board become, the more they tend to pull the board with them into staff work. If the purpose of giving management authority to the executive committee is to ensure that staff members follow the board's wishes, it is better for the board to figure out what its wishes are clearly enough that it can write them into policies. The executive committee can then review some staff decisions, not to approve or disapprove them but to decide whether they raise issues that need to be brought to the board.

For instance, the board might, by policy, allow the staff to shift up to five thousand dollars from one major section of the budget to another. Amounts from five thousand to ten thousand dollars would be reviewed by the executive committee, and amounts over ten thousand dollars would have to be approved by the full board. So the organ breaks. The administrator, working with the building staff (including the lay physical plant team), determines that the repair requires adjusting the music budget upward by eight thousand dollars. She finds the money in another section of the budget and includes the adjustments in her report to the executive committee. That is the end of the matter unless the executive committee decides that the board needs to think about a related policy or vision question (like "What style of music will best serve our congregation in the coming decade?"). With a process like this, most decisions can move forward under staff direction. Only policy questions and large dollar amounts go to the board, and the executive committee keeps the boundary firm.

Another group approach to management is to entrust ministry decision making to a "ministry leadership team." This group of three to five is not a subset of the board but part of the ministry staff structure, and leads the staff as a collective. The team may include only paid staff members, or it may include one or more lay members. In effect, this team is the innermost concentric circle of the staff. It might meet weekly; the whole staff, monthly; and a larger group, including lay ministry team leaders, once a quarter. A ministry leadership team meeting does many of the things good board meetings avoid—problem solving, arbitration, and case-by-case decision making.

For any collective or team leadership structure, it is important to address some sticky questions: What, exactly, does it mean to say, "The team decides"? Do team members vote? What happens in case of a tie? What happens when there is a need to fill a vacancy? Who deals with serious questions about a team member's performance? What does it mean to hold a team accountable? One way to deal with questions like these is to say that normally the team is expected to operate collegially or by consensus, but if that is not possible, the head of staff has the responsibility for making final decisions in the team's behalf.

Collective leadership probably tends to bias decision making in favor of the status quo, because the status quo is the fallback option if the team cannot agree on change. If the congregation means to continue following the basic strategies it followed in the past, this arrangement may be fine. Congregations that see the need for major change—if their community environment is changing, if cultural perspectives about faith are changing, if new generations define congregational success in new ways—then they may want to consider shifting to an individual staff leader. A congregation with a highly entrepreneurial clergy leader might risk the disadvantages of collective leadership to slow the process down a little!

In structuring the staff, especially in a small or midsize congregation, it is appropriate to consider the specific personalities involved. In a large corporation, it may make sense to say, "We don't design the job to fit the person," but even the largest congregations have small staffs by corporate standards. It makes sense to base the shape of the staff partly on the strengths of the individuals in place, anticipating that it will need to remain flexible as staff members come and go.

Evaluation Principles

Firm boundaries require that the board hold staff members accountable for their performance. Along with policies on delegation, the board needs to establish a strong practice of goal setting and evaluation. Many people flinch at the mention of evaluation, and with reason. Research shows that in many workplaces, evaluation actually hurts employee productivity by annually lowering morale. In congregations, staff evaluation often is conducted as a popularity poll with anonymous respondents rating staff performance on the basis of subjective impressions. In effect, the staff members answer to hundreds of semi-invisible bosses who can invent new things to blame them for at any time. This approach raises stress even for popular staff members and does little to improve performance.

Another reason to dislike staff evaluation is that people who are in conflict with a staff member often propose evaluation as a way to express unhappiness. For the staff, this ploy turns evaluation into a harbinger of doom, like the arrival of the priest in an old movie. Evaluation is a poor way to deal with conflict, whether the conflict is really about staff or (as is often the case when a staff member is criticized) the congregation itself is divided over an underlying issue. As a rule, it is better in a conflict to adhere strictly to the rules, policies, and procedures in place, rather than to try to change them. Policies adopted under stress make poor precedents, for the same reason that "great cases make bad law."

Understandably, some clergy and staff erect rigid boundaries around themselves and refuse to be evaluated or (more often) simply never get around to it. In frustration, boards sometimes insist on inappropriately punitive or quantitative systems of evaluation, in the hope of cracking down on what they see as poor performance. Such rigid, unilateral approaches rarely achieve the hoped-for outcome—safety for the barricaded staff member, efficiency for the harsh board member.

Despite the pitfalls, evaluation is important to effective partnership, from the board and head of staff on down. Firm boundaries require accountability, and accountability requires an atmosphere in which people give each other feedback. When evaluation is done well, it clears the air and motivates improvement. It can also sharpen awareness of differences between an individual's sense of calling and the congregation's emerging vision, leading to adjustment or even to separation. Although a unilateral decision to end a partnership is rarely easy, avoiding problems to postpone the pain makes it no easier. Regular evaluation helps to surface issues while the relationship is good enough to make it possible to work on them. Effective evaluation is

- *Scheduled:* Evaluation takes place by the calendar, not in response to problems.
- *Mutual:* Everyone gives and receives feedback.
- *Goal-centered:* Previously established goals are the basis for evaluation.
- *Individual:* Evaluation asks, "Am I meeting the expected standard for my job?" "How am I contributing to our goals?"
- *Collective:* "What progress have we made toward our goals?" "How do we need to adjust course?" "How are we fulfilling our vision for this particular program area?"
- *Backward looking:* "What did I accomplish?" "How well did we do?"
- *Forward looking:* "How can I improve?" "What should we do differently next time?"

Nothing can make evaluation easy all the time. Sometimes difficult words need to be said and heard. But with a healthy process, evaluation can help leaders pull together toward shared goals.

Annual Cycle of
Planning and Evaluation

Effective goal-setting and evaluation call for a comprehensive calendar. Figure 7.1 shows one way the sequence might be laid

Figure 7.1

GOAL-SETTING AND EVALUATION

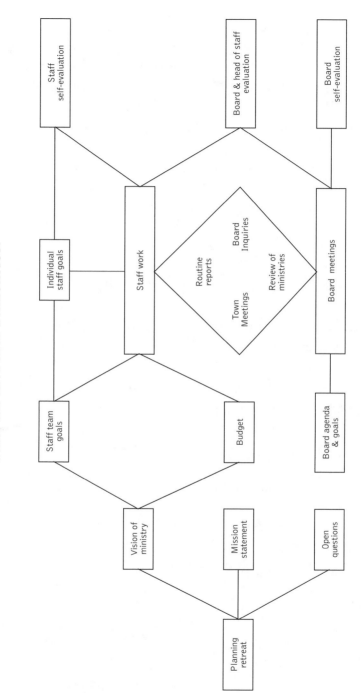

out. The upper part of the diagram shows staff activities, with the board's activities below. In the middle, on the level that begins with "planning retreat," are activities that fall into the zone of overlap between ministry and governance, where board and staff work together. In any congregation, the sequence needs to be coordinated with the fiscal year, officer elections, holidays, and other givens. In a congregation with a July 1 fiscal year, for instance, the planning retreat might happen in February, so that it can influence ministry plans and budgets for a program year that starts in September. Staff evaluations take place in the fall, and the board and head of staff evaluate each other in January. It is not necessary—or possible, usually—to schedule everything to dovetail logically. Evaluations do not have to happen after the end of a planning year—if there is a good reason, they can just as well come in the middle. Evaluation should always be based on previously agreed-upon plans, but there is no need for planning, budgeting, evaluation, and election years to synchronize in any special way.

A key event for goal setting and evaluation is the annual planning retreat. Typically, this event includes the board and senior members of the staff, including lay staff as appropriate. Ideally, the group spends at least a day and a half off-site with a strict no-cell-phone rule. The agenda varies from year to year; the focus is always on discernment and strategy, the two zones of responsibility shared by board and staff. Some special attention to the mission is appropriate every year—but it is rarely a good use of time to tweak the wording of the mission statement that often. Once every five years is more than enough, unless something is terribly wrong with the existing statement.

Vision of Ministry

A more necessary work product from the retreat and related activities is the annual vision of ministry, defined in chapter 5 as an answer to the question, "In what new and different ways will we transform lives in the next one to three years?" To put it differently, the vision of ministry is the board's short list of priorities.

Why a short list? Because when a list of priorities is long, they're not priorities! The vision of ministry is a short list of things the board means to accomplish, no matter what. The fact that something does not make the list does not mean that it won't happen. While creating the vision, the board will bank a number of ideas for the future: pieces of a long-term vision to which the board is not prepared to make an ironclad commitment now. There is no way to do this without sometimes saying no.

The exact process for creating the vision of ministry will change from year to year. In some years, the ministry priorities may be so obvious that the board creates the vision quickly and uses the planning retreat for other purposes. Most of the time, the vision of ministry emerges from a yearlong conversation, followed by deeper reflection and exchange during the retreat.

Board members schooled in the SMART system of goal-setting (Specific, Measurable, Actionable, Realistic, and Timely) may make the mistake of letting these considerations influence the vision process too soon. Concern for measurement, raised too early, can inhibit boards from saying what they mean. Many things a congregation properly wants are hard to measure. Often the more accurately you state the congregation's mission, the less precisely you can measure its success. In youth programs, for example, it is easy to measure registration, attendance, dropout rates, and dollars raised. A little harder to measure—but more important—are such things as the number of volunteer hours given and young people's specific knowledge about Scripture and tradition. The most difficult of all to measure are the actual outcomes of a ministry with youth: ethical life choices, faith commitment, lifelong service, and adult observance and affiliation. The board should not limit its vision of ministry to outcomes that are easy to measure. Instead, it should say what it envisions as exactly as it can and leave it to the staff to figure out a way to measure it. Measurement does not have to be strictly quantitative—and for most religious goals, it can't be. John Carver put it well: "A crude measure of the right thing beats a precise measure of the wrong thing."[2]

Open Questions

In addition to a vision of ministry, the planning retreat produces "open questions." In discussing the congregation's work and drawing out the hopes and worries of its leaders, retreat participants may find technical challenges surfacing that all but suggest their own solutions. If the boiler is broken, you fix it. If the secretary quits, you hire another. Other challenges—developmental ones—require a longer process. You can see the road ahead; if there is a tunnel, you can see light at the end of it, and you have a good idea what life will be like once you get there. A building project is often like that. So is updating a successful but stale program for young adults. Technical and developmental challenges are good candidates for the annual vision of ministry.

Other challenges—frame bending or adaptive challenges—do not lend themselves to quick or even slow decision making. Perhaps your congregation needs to decide whether to abandon, renovate, or replace a building that has been the main symbol of its identity for 150 years. Or you may wonder how to serve a neighborhood whose residents are different from the people of your congregation. You may have a nagging sense, as Jonah did, that God is calling you to make radical changes, but the subject is too hot to push it to decision making. The board could make up its mind and announce a solution prematurely, but that seems likely to increase division rather than encourage movement toward a decision. With such challenges, the board can make a major contribution simply by stating the issue clearly as an open question— one it expects the congregation to decide sometime in the future, but not now. For now, the next step is sustained, reflective, and inclusive conversation.

Open questions often raise anxiety, so it is important not to raise too many at a time. It can be helpful to give some idea of when a decision is likely to be made, who will make it, and what opportunities members of the congregation will have for input. Drawing such perimeters around an open question helps to reduce anxiety, making it easier for members to participate in civil and constructive dialogue.

Keeping one or two open questions before the congregation helps the congregation to see its board as open to influence. A congregational meeting organized around an open question can be expected to attract more interest than the usual elections, officer reports, and budgets. Plans and visions are important; questions are potentially transforming. Don't be afraid, as leaders, to admit that you don't have all the answers.

Staff Goals

After the retreat, everyone has work to do. The staff needs to translate the board's vision of ministry into goals and objectives. In larger churches, the senior staff has goals of its own. Even a simple common slogan, like "We will integrate social outreach into everything we do," can be a good counter to the tendency of busy staff members to draw back into their departments. The staff's goals take the board's vision of ministry and move it to a more practical level. If the vision of ministry says, "We will make room to welcome more people," the staff might say, "After the first of the year, we will add a second session to our children's Sunday school. By then we will be ready to double the number of parking-lot greeters skilled at hospitality to families with children." And so on. Setting staff goals right after the planning retreat helps to ensure that they will be consistent with the board's priorities, expressed in the vision of ministry. The staff leader will play a strong role in deciding on staff goals and may have authority to make a decision if consensus can't be reached. The nature of congregational work, though, makes consensus a desirable outcome; it's hard to motivate people if all you have is sticks and carrots!

Individual staff members set goals next. As anyone who works for a congregation quickly learns, each staff member belongs to at least two groups that are in tension with each other at least some of the time. One is the staff team and its leader. The other is the natural constituency that surrounds every staff position, from senior clergy to custodian. Managing this tension is an important key to success for staff members, especially when setting goals. The supporters of a ministry area can be fierce partisans for a particular perception of reality. For staff members who share their vantage point—be it the choir loft, the religious-education wing, or the boiler room—it can be seductive to fall in with the group, especially when its members are complaining. "The old people want to impose an outdated standard of child behavior." "Ministers care only about the words, never the music." "We're running a surplus all right, if you ignore the leaky roof." Beginning each staff member's goal-setting conversation with the board's vision of ministry and the goals set by senior staff helps put parochial concerns into the context of the wider mission. It is the job of every ministry team leader to set the stage for goal setting in this way. Then the team proceeds to set goals for itself, and the staff member (in consultation with his or her team, supervisor, and colleagues) sets goals for himself or herself. A practice that promotes a sense of permission and autonomy among teams and their leaders is to presume that their goals will be consistent with the board and senior staff goals, and to deal only with exceptions, instead of sending all goals up the line to be approved.

Board Goals

The board is not exempt from post-retreat goal setting. Having endorsed a vision of ministry for the congregation as a whole, it needs to set goals and an agenda for its own work. This is the time to establish a twelve-month plan for board meetings, giving each meeting a major focus. This practice not only helps the board members to resist micromanagement; it makes it possible for them to create ad hoc committees to plan some of the meetings. These groups may organize a wider gathering of members in advance of the board meeting—for example, they might gather parents of nursery children—to provide input to the board's consideration of a program area. Or they might bring in an outside expert, someone from another congregation with a different approach to the same challenge, or some data about demographic changes. When the board meets, its conversation will be fed.

Some of the board's goals may have to do with its own process and disciplines. It may decide, for instance, to create a covenant of expectations for board members or to implement one of the other practices described in chapter 6. A goal might be to make sure every board member has a basic understanding of the congregation's finances. Whatever goals the board decides upon, it builds into a yearlong plan for its agenda.

The Budget

The budget, like staff and board goals, translates the board's vision of ministry into specifics. Unfortunately, many congregations draw up budgets through a process that has little relation to their vision.

Congregational budget makers frequently divide into two camps that approach the task in different ways. The first camp is likely to include children of the Great Depression, experts in finance, elementary-school teachers, and people anxious about their own financial situation. Their first priority is to make sure that the budget balances and that the congregation makes no plans or commitments it is less that 100 percent certain it can meet. They squint over budget sheets like bookkeepers of old with their bright lamps and sleeve garters—I call this camp the Green Eyeshades.

The second camp typically includes young clergy, upscale decorators, baby boomers, college professors, and commission salespeople. They firmly believe that with God (or even without), all things are possible. They say, "We are a congregation, not a business." This camp can be identified at budget meetings mostly by their absence. When lassoed into talking about money, they glaze over. Staring at a distant sunrise, they float over the surface of numerical reality—I call them the Rose-Colored Glasses.

The division between the Eyeshades and the Rosy Glasses is as old as Mary and Martha, Moses and Aaron, Job and Job's wife. It is as deeply rooted in our culture as the duality of secular and sacred, temporal and spiritual. There is nothing wrong with it, so long as both groups value the other's contributions and see themselves as members of one team. But too often, the boundary becomes rigid—one group always thinks of ways to spend more money; the other always calculates the reasons why we can't afford it.

The budget process often sets up friction between the Glasses and the Eyeshades. Typically, the first step is to ask program units to request a budget for next year. The program units (full of rosy thinkers) ask for more than they expect and then some. Finance committee folk (strapping on their eyeshades) put all of the requests onto a spreadsheet as a "dream budget." Usually even the dream budget ends up trimmed, so that it resembles the Green Eyeshades' own, fiscally sound dreams.

The fund drive, predictably, falls short of the "dream" goal. How could it not? Calling a goal a dream almost guarantees that you'll fall short. The finance committee sharpens its pencils and begins grinding the dream down to a practical nub.

The program people rise up, asking, "How can we say we can't afford what God has called us to accomplish?" The finance people answer, "Good stewards live within their means." The Eyeshades with their pencils and spreadsheets do battle with the Rosy Glasses with their blunt-end scissors, opera glasses, and pink feathers. Eventually, together, they come up with a budget, but there has to be a better way!

A better way begins with the vision of ministry, understood as the first draft of the budget, though it may contain no numbers at all. The vision of ministry confronts the question most budget debates address only indirectly: Which aspects of our mission will be top priorities this year? After the board adopts it (usually at a formally called meeting after the retreat), along with the board's fiscal policies, the vision of ministry becomes the basis for the call for proposed budgets from the program units. The request is not for a "dream" budget, but for a budget that will accomplish the vision of ministry and comply with the fiscal policies.

The budget itself may be assembled by a finance committee and presented to the board for approval. A better process, though, is to put responsibility for creating the budget in the same place as responsibility for achieving the vision of ministry: the staff. At the very least, the head of staff should be required to sign off on the budget, saying to the board, "I believe this budget is a reasonable plan to achieve our vision." Or not. In many congregations the budget process sails right from the committees to the board without the clergy leader (or other head of staff) even having to express an opinion. Under that procedure, it is a stretch to hold the head of staff accountable for much of anything.

With a budget created in this way, the annual fund drive can be based on the vision of ministry as well. Contributors are asked for amounts that, if most of them say "yes," will make the vision possible. The board, clergy, and staff make it clear that the vision is not just something they hope to shoot for; it's a goal they mean to reach. Year after year, people learn that when the congregation asks for gifts, it means what it says. If the members give what is asked, the results promised—the vision of lives changed through ministry—will happen.

Board Work, Staff Work

The planning retreat, vision of ministry, and goal setting by the staff and board lay the foundation for a rich year's work. Chapter 6 described many aspects of the board's ongoing work; the diamond-shaped section of figure 7.1 shows some of the activities that contribute to board-staff partnership.

Routine reports from the staff (including lay leaders of ministry programs) appear for the most part in the board packet. In setting standards for the packet, the board may wish to emphasize that reports should focus on how the work does or does not fulfill the vision of ministry.

Board inquiries are simply that. The board may ask the staff to give advice or generate reports to help the board to monitor compliance with board policies or to support the board's reflections about policy or vision. The whole board can ask for information from the staff—but the right of individual board members to do so should be limited. A simple policy to prevent individual board members from distracting staff with time-consuming inquiries is simply to empower the head of staff to say no. The member can then take the matter up with the full board.

The board's agenda includes *scheduled reviews* of ministries or groups of ministries. Board reviews are not the time to evaluate the performance of staff members; it is a chance for the board to talk in depth about the congregation's work in an important aspect of its mission. When boundaries are clear, the board and ministry leaders can talk about program details without risk that the board will yield to the temptation to decide what the staff should be deciding. Immersion in details is valuable preparation for the board's work of discernment, strategy, and oversight. As preparation for a board review of social ministries, for instance, members might agree that each board member will volunteer at least once in the month before the meeting in an outreach ministry new to him or her. Testimony about the personal meaning of the experience can be the basis for the spiritual prelude to a substantive discussion about how the congregation means to transform lives through ministry in the community.

Town meetings are gatherings of the congregation to discuss open questions or other topics of importance. Such gatherings should never happen simply to "sell" members on the board's prior decisions. An authentic element of listening needs to be included, or the congregation will quickly lose trust in the board's openness to influence. It helps to ask the board members present to identify themselves, so that participants know whom they can speak to if they have afterthoughts. Recording important points from the conversation confirms that the board is listening as well. Town meetings are a good occasion to use the congregation's talent pool of skilled facilitators, or even (especially for "hot" issues) to engage an outside leader. Like the board's own conversations about open questions, a town meeting is enriched by new information—not so much that it takes the whole time to absorb it, but enough to stimulate a fresh take on the topic.

After a town meeting, the board feeds back, in writing, to the congregation what it heard. When it makes a decision, it references the results of the town meeting in the report. Even those whose input did not carry the day are reassured by the clear sign that the board listened.

Evaluation

As the last stage of the cycle—not necessarily exactly one year after setting goals, but annually—the staff members evaluate themselves and one another. Staff evaluations need to be conducted with great care to protect the dignity and morale of staff members. Each staff member's direct supervisor takes responsibility for the evaluation process and report. For hourly-wage staff, the evaluation process should be as private as possible, consistent with gathering appropriate input. For program staff leaders, the supervisor might enlist key ministry team leaders in an evaluation session. The senior staff team might also engage in group evaluation. In every case, the individual staff member and his or her direct supervisor sit down for a conversation about how the work is going. This is a chance for the supervisor to express appreciation for the staff member's contributions and to lay the groundwork for goal setting in the coming year.

The board, by policy, requires the staff to engage in evaluation, but the staff owns its own process. The "customer" for staff evaluations is not the board or a committee but the staff leadership, beginning with the direct supervisor in each case and ending with the head of staff. Others can and should participate by giving input, and for senior staff a summary report of the results may be appropriately shared with the board or others. Raw data from a survey about staff performance should not be published; doing so empowers the least constructive respondents to have disproportionate impact on morale.

The head of staff, in addition to participating in evaluation with the senior staff team, evaluates and is evaluated by the board, and the board evaluates itself. The governance committee, if there is one, structures the board's process each year. Each member might complete a written self-evaluation of his or her performance as a board member. The questionnaire might also ask about the member's contribution to achieving board goals set the previous year. Some boards also ask each member to rate every other member. The committee tallies the results and gives each member both an individual report and a summary of all responses. On the day of the evaluation, board members meet in groups of three to talk about the performance of each as a board member during the year. The governance committee gathers the results of this discussion, including any items that might inform future adjustments to the board covenant or board goals for the coming year.

Having had this conversation, the board will be in a good frame of mind for its evaluation conversation with the head of staff. One way to start is with written input from each member and the head of staff by asking simple questions about what they need from one another, what they are grateful for, and where they would like something different. The governance committee summarizes the responses, leads a conversation, and writes a brief report of major comments and concerns. If others report directly to the board, the board engages in a similar process for each of them.

When the head of staff is also the clergy leader, it is appropriate to have a more complete performance evaluation once every three years or so. Because the clergy leader role extends well beyond the board, a wider process is appropriate. One approach is for the board to appoint a small committee of highly trusted members, with approval of each member by the clergy leader and the board. This committee takes responsibility for deciding how to gather data and input, and for writing the report of the evaluation process. The report should not magnify complaints, sweep widespread concerns under the rug, or forget to pass along appreciation.[3]

Congregations have important work to do, and they can't afford the luxury of boards and staff that hold each other in a barren stalemate. The most effective way to manage daily ministry in congregations larger than 150 active members is through a professional staff that coordinates the work of volunteers in ministry. The board, staff, and congregation together articulate the mission, choose strategies, and select a vision of ministry. By adopting generous policies on delegation, the board enables the staff to lead the congregation in achieving ministry results without needing to stop continually for approvals, second-guessing, and advice. The board monitors the work continually, and reserves the power to intervene—but in the normal course of business, its evaluations, like its goals, follow a yearly cycle. With firm boundaries between their spheres, the board and staff achieve a partnership that lets each make its best and highest contribution.

8 ∷ Exploring
Governance Change

One approach to changing the organizational structure of a congregation is to reprogram it like a computer. The board appoints a committee, which goes into seclusion like a group of old-time hackers in a garage. The group members scour the Internet for free resources, read some books about the latest new ideas, and punch out a set of bylaw changes and a new organization chart. Then they roll out version 1.0 of their proposal. Like version 1.0 of anything, it turns out to have bugs in it. Some congregations simply reject the changes. Others, like so many users of new software, vote them in, only to experience incompatibilities or crashes later on.

A congregation is not a machine; it is a living system. As such, it has a strong inclination to persist in doing what has become familiar. In a plant or animal, biologists call this inclination homeostasis, from the Greek for "staying the same." In organizational systems, the unwritten law is, "When we don't know what to do, we do what we know." The imposition of good ideas from outside is not enough to cause a congregation and its leaders to modify ingrained daily habits. Systems can be extremely clever about undermining anyone or anything that tries to change them from outside. On the other hand, a system can change itself quite readily in response to inner forces. It may change in response to the shared unhappiness of its leaders. It may change to achieve the same old results in a new situation. Or it may change because it catches an exciting glimpse of new results—results that fit so powerfully its inward sense of mission as to disturb old comforts and make the status quo untenable. Bylaw amendments may be necessary for systemic change, but they are definitely not enough. The secret to intentional change is to engage the system's own deepest motivations—including its resistance to change. A system changes willingly when it sees change as a necessary way to continue being what it truly is.

Overview of the Governance Change Process

A change process like the one shown in figure 8.1 stands a better chance of producing systemic change than an approach focused on changing the bylaws or the organization chart. This process has been tested by a variety of congregations, each of which has carried it out differently. It takes longer than most people expect, because it aims to change both structure and behavior, roles and attitudes, language and understandings. Systemic change requires wide participation and starts by asking questions rather than by providing answers. We will begin with a brief overview of the process, than walk through it step by step.

Instead of a bylaws-revision committee, this process begins with a leadership retreat. At the retreat, leaders talk about what they value in their current structure, what they find difficult or frustrating, and what they hope for from a new way of organizing. Someone presents a change process adapted from figure 8.1 and describes some possible alternative outcomes—with the assurance that change will come only when the leadership supports it. A presentation of the concepts in chapters 3 and 4 provides shared language for leaders to use as they consider alternatives. By the end of the retreat, participants should be able to produce two things: a list of their concerns and aspirations for the congregation's governance, and a recommendation to the board of whether to

Figure 8.1

GOVERNANCE CHANGE PROCESS TIMELINE

Year 1	1	Appoint retreat planning team
	2	Leadership retreat on governance
	3	Appoint governance task force (GTF)
	4	GTF listening process with congregation
	5	GTF presents governance vision to board for endorsement
	6	GTF engages in "iterative process" of policy writing:
	7	GTF drafts a group of policies
	8	Board reviews and affirms policies
	9	GTF seeks board input on an open question
	10	GTF seeks wider review and input
	11	GTF revises policies, repeats the process
	12	Board adopts proposed policy book for the trial run
Year 2	1	Trial run begins
	2	
	3	Periodic evaluation and review
	4	
	5	Possible tweaking of policies
	6	
	7	Leadership retreat: vision of ministry & open questions
	8	
	9	Evaluation of trial run
	10	Set vision of ministry and staff goals for Year 3
	11	Approvals to make the new structure permanent
	12	GTF disbands
Year 3	1	Governance committee takes over monitoring
	2	
	3	
	4	Continuing self-evaluation and review
	5	
	6	
	7	
	8	
	9	Routine annual evaluations as required by new policies
	10	Set vision of ministry and staff goals for Year 4
	11	
	12	
Year 4		Continue the new structure and process

initiate a change process. If the group decides not to proceed with a full governance change process, it may produce a list of ideas for improving the existing structure or practicing it better.

If, after the retreat, leaders agree to continue, they appoint a governance task force (GTF), which fashions a proposal step by step—drafting first an overall statement of the goals of the governance change, then a general structure, then top-level board policies in a logical sequence. At each step, the GTF reports back to the board and senior staff and asks for affirmation (not adoption) of its work to date. Affirmation is a yellow light—permission to share the partial proposal with a wider group of leaders, then with all interested members. At each iteration, the GTF makes changes in response to widely held concerns and shares a revised draft with the board. Repeatedly along the way, the GTF explains the process to the whole congregation, so that everyone can know what changes are under discussion, who will decide about them and when, and what opportunities members will have for input in the meantime.

Once enough policies have been developed by the GTF and affirmed by the board to provide a reasonable safety net, the GTF asks the board (and the board may ask the congregation) to approve a year's trial run of the new structure. The GTF coaches and monitors the trial and, toward the end of the year, leads an evaluation. If the evaluation is positive, the GTF presents the structure (with any adjustments made along the way) for final approval. Only at this point are bylaws or other documents amended as required to make the changes permanent.

At this point, the GTF disbands, but the process is not finished. For some time, reverting to the old behavior is a continual temptation for leaders—especially when they become anxious. Leaders find the new ways awkward and continually discover situations in which the new structure calls for behavior that surprises them, because they have not thought the implications through. After the

GTF dissolves, a board governance committee takes over its work of monitoring, training, and evaluation, as described in chapter 6. Real evaluations can now take place, because at this point the system has operated for a year under pre-established goals. Making the new behavior automatic takes, on average, yet another year. At that point—four years from the beginning of the process—leaders' first thought, most of the time, should be to follow the new structure rather than the old one. Enculturation of new leaders, updating of covenants, and the shoring up of effective practice when it sags—these tasks remain on the board's and staff's agenda indefinitely.

Now that we have seen the governance change process in overview, we will start again and walk through the process more deliberately, beginning with the process before the process—deciding whether it is a good time to be considering a change in governance at all.

Questions to Ask before Starting

Governance change is not always a good idea. There is no perfect time, to be sure, but sometimes it is a good idea to wait. Before you dive into a governance change process, here are some questions you might ask that will help determine whether this is a good time:

Who wants this change? Before moving ahead with a change process, you need support from a significant group of lay leaders and staff. If your clergy leader is strongly committed to continuing your current structure, it is not constructive to begin a process that is likely to increase demand for a new one.

If the main reason you are interested in governance change is that one person (especially if that person is the clergy leader) read this book, the next step is obviously to buy more copies! One of the hazards of reading a book or going to a seminar is that you can find yourself alone in your enthusiasm. Another hazard is to become so convinced of a specific "model" that you have a hard time listening to others who are just starting to consider the question. It is important to tell others why you are initiating a change process, but it is even more important to gain a broad base of support by listening to others.

Admittedly, if you wait for throngs to rise up and demand a governance change process, you will wait a long time. But if only two or three of you want change, that's not enough. If interest in restructuring is lukewarm, it might be best to initiate some education or self-examination, rather than a full process. You might want to hold a "discussion that is only a discussion" for leaders to talk about what is going well in your decision-making process now and what they would like to improve. Some of the ideas presented below for the initial leadership retreat work equally well for a pre-retreat meeting. Agreement about the outcome or goals of a change process is not necessary or desirable; at this stage, all that is needed is agreement that a process is appropriate and timely.

Why is this question coming up now? Sometimes when leaders are in conflict, they decide that structure is the problem and hope that a change will make things better for them. If the conflict is severe enough to involve rudeness, personal attacks, or secret meetings, it is best to address the conflict first. Otherwise, some people will see the governance change process as a stealthy way to get the upper hand—and they may be right! Any time the question of governance arises as a way to resolve differences over clergy or staff members, or about worship, social issues, or building policy, is best to resolve the conflict under the existing rules before thinking about governance change. Rebuilding a boat while it is sailing is difficult; rebuilding it while it is on fire or when a mutiny is under way is pretty much impossible.

What else is on our agenda in the coming year or two? If you have a building program coming up, or you need to make challenging decisions soon about worship, morality, or social justice, that would be a caution sign. A congregation can have only two or three big things on its agenda at a time. Governance may need to wait its turn.

On the other hand, if your clergy leader is supportive, it is *not* necessarily a caution sign if he or she is close to retirement, is about to go on a sabbatical, or is with you as a one- or two-year interim leader while you search. Such moments in a congregation's life are opportunities to rethink the lay-clergy partnership while the partners have some space in their togetherness. In the case of a sabbatical, the scope and general direction of the proposed change should be agreed upon before the clergy leader leaves. If agreement cannot be reached, the process should be suspended. Conversation may continue (how could it not?), but no decisions are made until after the sabbatical.

During an interim, coordination with the search committee is essential, so that prospective candidates know that a change process is under way and how it might affect the clergy leadership role they are considering. It is much better to begin a change process during the interim than to spring it on a leader chosen for a role that is about to change.

When did we last reorganize? How do people feel about that process and its outcomes? If the congregation still holds bad feelings from its last bylaws revision process, it is helpful to put those feelings to rest before starting something new. In the last reorganization, one person or a small group of members may have created and proposed a set of bylaw changes. With pride of authorship, they put their work before the congregation only to see it bent, folded, mutilated, and rejected—or adopted in a form that did not leave them feeling good. After such a process, some people may want to revisit the original bylaw proposal, while others have learned to associate reorganization with tiresome parliamentary debates or other unpleasantness and want to avoid the subject altogether.

Most of these cautions are merely that—yellow lights that may or may not indicate the need to postpone governance change. If your current structure discourages initiative, abuses volunteers, or contributes to a morbid sense of drift, the question is not whether to explore changing it, but when.

Preparing the Way

When the time is right, a good way to begin thinking about governance is to gather leaders for a retreat to educate them about governance and to take stock of their interest in exploring governance change. In preparation for the retreat, the board appoints an advance committee. The advance committee's job is to plan a process for deciding whether to have a process. As with many important decisions, appointing an advance committee helps to avoid the common problem of appointing a team to formulate and push a proposal that is ultimately turned down. (One advance committee called itself "the John the Baptist committee" and cried out from time to time that it was *not* the governance committee.)

As always with retreats, the ideal is to meet away from the usual haunts—where if the phone rings, it's not for you. (For the same reason, a clear agreement to limit cell-phone use is a good idea.) Staying overnight helps separate the retreat from daily work and fosters flexibility of thinking. These benefits are hard to imagine ahead of time, but they can make a big difference. As a retreat facilitator, I have often heard board members say, "I voted against spending the money to meet off-site. But I was wrong. This retreat will pay for itself many times over."

Speaking of money, hiring a consultant to facilitate can be a big help. Be sure, though, that you know how your consultant will approach the task. Some consultants promote only one specific system of board governance; all consultants worth considering have ideas about what works and what doesn't. You will want to know that your consultant's ideas are compatible with yours and that he or she can listen with respect to the ideas of others. For your initial leadership retreat, you will want a facilitator who can strike a balance between *process* (letting you have your own discussion without pushing a narrow agenda) and *content* (offering language and ideas that will help you have a better conversation). Perhaps the most helpful trait to look for in a consultant is curiosity—about your congregation and its history, values, and traditions, and about the hopes and expectations your leaders bring to the governance discussion. It is better to muddle awkwardly through your own conversation than to be force-marched expertly through someone else's.

A Leadership Retreat

At the retreat, starting with some mixer or team-building activities helps introduce newcomers to the group and creates a comfortable atmosphere for everyone to participate. Prayer, text study, singing, and ritual—as appropriate to your tradition—help place the work of the retreat in a larger picture. Such practices remind participants that in every time and place, people have strived to gather worshiping communities in just, effective, up-to-date ways. Some personal sharing helps to recognize the unique experiences that color each participant's perceptions about leadership, decision making, money, and power. "Opening the room," so that all ideas are heard with respect, builds trust.

Before talking about change, it is good to spend some time describing the status quo. The "Board Time Analysis" activity described in appendix A helps leaders look at how the board spends its time now. Using old minutes (or memory) leaders estimate how much of the board's time is spent on management decisions, reports, and other matters. Sometimes in the course of this activity, it turns out that board members describe the board's current practice differently from one another. Rather than pushing to resolve differences, explore the reasons for the different perceptions. Your board may have changed, and leaders' perceptions may be drawn from different eras. Or current and past board leaders may feel defensive in the face of what feels like criticism. A reminder that the whole board shares responsibility for its practice can help to take leaders off the spot. The time-analysis exercise produces data that can be used later in evaluating any changes, so be sure to save it. It may also produce consensus about areas in which the board might like to spend more or less time, or routine activities that others wish the board would do or stop doing. These, too, can be recorded and saved for the last, decision-making phase of the retreat.

It can be fun to break up into groups and ask each group to draw an organization chart for the congregation as it actually operates. An organization chart should answer certain questions about each position; for example, Who appoints someone to do this job? Who is responsible for making sure someone does it properly? Who can fire the person? Who approves the necessary resources—money, building space, and staff? After the groups have finished, have them post and present their charts. Enjoy the differences rather than trying to reconcile them. Look at each chart appreciatively—as a source of information about how people see and describe the congregation.

Including an educational component in the retreat plan adds grist to what to some participants might otherwise seem a tiresome diet of pure "process." Someone might prepare to present your polity tradition in comparison with others. Edward Long's *Patterns of Polity* may help the presenter identify the core values of your own denomination's style of governance. Other presentations could be based on chapters 3 and 4 of this book or on one of the resources found in the bibliography. Another presentation might include information about your congregation's size and its history of growth and decline. How might those changes account for your current structure? Present some information about size based on the "Size Matters" section of chapter 1, and on resources like Alice Mann's *Raising the Roof* and *The In-Between Church*. Are you organized to be larger or smaller than you are? If there is a mismatch, is it intentional or just a leftover? Asking people to prepare presentations is a good way to make sure a variety of voices are heard and to ensure broad acceptance of decisions made at the retreat.

To help participants look ahead, a presentation based on the conceptual maps in chapter 4 and the roles of the board in chapter 5 can be helpful. Be sure to emphasize that the proposed process is an open one, designed to enable your congregation to create a structure suitable to its needs and traditions. Pay attention to the points that draw particularly strong positive or negative responses.

Wind up the retreat by seeing if participants can agree on a rough "statement of wishes" for the congregation's governance. Then ask, "How big a change is this? Is it worth a full governance process?" Share a plan for a full governance process like the one in figure 8.1, and explain why major shifts in the behavior of a system take a longer time and broader participation to achieve. See if the participants can come to consensus about what kinds of improvements they want in the congregation's governance and how big a process they want to initiate. The advance committee writes up the results of the retreat, which become part of the board's agenda at its next official meeting.

Members of the board on the advance team may take a strict view of your denominational polity—assuming, in effect, that only what is customary is permitted. If possible, set these concerns aside for now and say what you want to do, leaving questions about how to harmonize your plans with polity rulebooks for later. Even the most prescriptive polities allow more flexibility than people sometimes assume.

Governance Task Force

Assuming that the board decides to go ahead with a full governance change process, its next task is to appoint a governance task force (GTF). The choice of personnel for this group is crucial. All of the GTF members must have the congregation's trust and must be able to set aside preconceptions and factional loyalties if they are to participate in a truly open process. Here is a good method for appointing the GTF—or any group that needs wide trust and respect to fulfill its purpose:

The chair or other process leader first introduces or reviews the concept of brainstorming (all ideas are welcome; no criticism, praise, or "improving on" ideas is allowed). Then, using newsprint, the board brainstorms a list of qualities the GTF will need. Close the brainstorming session, and discuss which items on the list are most important and generally agreed upon. Edit the list accordingly. Then assign board members the homework of coming to the next meeting with one or more potential nominees in mind. Urge members *not* to ask permission from the nominees, but simply to nominate the best. Any member may bring any number of nominations; all are encouraged to bring at least one.

After the meeting, send out the list of qualities to board members by e-mail, with a reminder of the homework assignment. Send another reminder ahead of the next board meeting. At the next meeting, pass out three-by-five cards, ask the members to write the name of each nominee on a separate card, and ask a teller team to tally all the nominations on a list. If someone gets more than one nomination, show the number, but list the names in random or alphabetical order. Discuss (maybe initially in subgroups, if there are more than twelve board members) what group of four—plus the clergy leader—would make the best GTF. When the board has agreed on a set of nominees (with perhaps an alternate or two), it charges one of its members with inviting the people to serve. Nominees should be told how they were chosen and shown the board's list of desired qualities and a written description of the GTF's task before deciding whether to accept the nomination.

Boards that use this process often experience a rate of acceptance that surprises them!

Planning the Process

The GTF's first job is to plan the process it will follow. The plan should specify the areas of governance that will be looked at, the concerns or goals to be addressed, the occasions when leaders or members can have input, the approximate date the task group's recommendations will be acted on, and the body that will act. It is worth mentioning the hope that, by the time of the final decision, every interested person will have had a chance to express his or her hopes and concerns, so that the vote itself will be an anticlimax. After it has drafted a proposed process, the GTF presents it to the board for approval.

Once the process is approved, the GTF publicizes it widely and repeatedly. It is always good to overdo publicity. People will accept a great deal of decision making by leaders if they are told well in advance—and reminded frequently—what is under consideration, when they can have input, who will decide, and when.

Setting the Vision

After securing approval of the process, the GTF articulates as well as it can the purpose of the governance change process. As a starting point, it has the "statement of wishes" from the leadership retreat. After reflecting on this document, the GTF presents a vision statement for the governance process. One church's GTF described its vision this way:

> The congregation of the ———— Church elects a board to function as its governing body and a minister to serve as its spiritual, programmatic, and administrative leader. The intended style of leadership will be consultative, collegial, and inclusive. Clarity about ultimate responsibility and authority will exist along with a democratic and egalitarian spirit. All church leaders are expected to practice transparent decision making, healthy conflict management, and mutual support in their respective roles.

After the board approves the vision, the GTF facilitates a series of sessions for the congregation at large and for specific groups of leaders. Presentations on governance alternatives, denominational wisdom, and best practices from the nonprofit world are mixed with liberal amounts of time for feedback and discussion. Periodically the GTF meets with the board to ask for affirmation of its work to date, and to share questions with which it is still struggling.

Iterative Decision Making

The cycle of GTF reflection, board affirmation, and wider conversations is what computer programmers call "iterative": the first round produces a result, which becomes the starting point for the next round, and so on.[1] The final product is a set of top-level policies that will become the basis for the board's policy book.

The governance vision that the board has already affirmed becomes the preamble to the policies on governance. After that, there is no one best sequence for drafting policies; each congregation finds different sticking points and has to find its way. I usually suggest starting with the management section of the policy book (see appendix B), especially the policies on delegation, followed by the oversight section. Discernment and strategy sections can be populated tentatively with whatever mission and vision statements and strategic plans already exist. Otherwise they can safely be left blank, to be filled in by the board during the trial run and afterward.

The iterative process (shown in figure 8.2) goes like this: The GTF drafts a set of policies (initially those describing the overall governance philosophy reached at the leadership retreat, then the policies on delegation, staff structure, oversight, and so on), and sends them to the board well in advance of its next meeting. Along with the proposed policies, the GTF sends background materials explaining the rationale for the recommendation and offering some considerations related to the question.

At the board meeting, the GTF presents its proposed policies. The board, which has read and reflected on the policies in advance, gives feedback and chooses either to "affirm" the policies or not. Affirmation does not freeze the text or put the policies

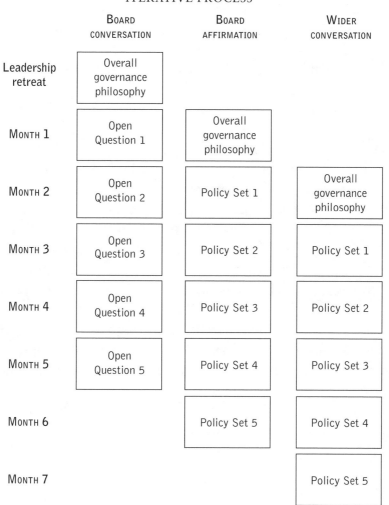

Figure 8.2

ITERATIVE PROCESS

	BOARD CONVERSATION	BOARD AFFIRMATION	WIDER CONVERSATION
Leadership retreat	Overall governance philosophy		
MONTH 1	Open Question 1	Overall governance philosophy	
MONTH 2	Open Question 2	Policy Set 1	Overall governance philosophy
MONTH 3	Open Question 3	Policy Set 2	Policy Set 1
MONTH 4	Open Question 4	Policy Set 3	Policy Set 2
MONTH 5	Open Question 5	Policy Set 4	Policy Set 3
MONTH 6		Policy Set 5	Policy Set 4
MONTH 7			Policy Set 5

into force. It gives the GTF permission to present the policies to a wider audience before—perhaps—revising them further. If the board declines to affirm the draft policies, the GTF revises and presents them again the next month. Nothing is presented to the wider audience that has not been affirmed by the board. This procedure avoids confusion in the congregation, which will tend to assume that the board is in at least general support of anything its committee (the GTF) presents more widely. It also provides a safe "container" for the board's conversation. Boards are more willing to be imaginative if they are not continually threatened with having to defend ideas they have not fully absorbed themselves.

As a separate step, the GTF shares an open question at each board meeting. An open question (like those discussed in chapter 7 in connection with evaluation) is a question for which the GTF has not yet reached an answer, which it is asking the board to discuss for a few minutes so the GTF can learn by listening. Typically the open question relates to the next set of policies the GTF plans to present for affirmation. The open question is presented and explained to the board with the request, "We are still struggling with this issue, and we would like to hear you talk about it for ten minutes, to help us in our thinking." The board is not encouraged to reach a conclusion or to give the GTF direction on the open question. At the board's next monthly meeting, the GTF returns, having adjusted its proposed policies (including, possibly, those previously affirmed by the board) and repeats the process. With each iteration, the GTF comes closer to the completion of its task.

An iterative process has several virtues. It honors the role of the GTF as imaginers-in-chief. It enables the board to play an important role in shaping the new structure in a reasonable amount of time. Sharing open questions elicits more helpful feedback from the board than could be obtained by presenting finished work. It keeps the process transparent to the membership without needlessly worrying people about alternatives unlikely to be chosen or confusing them about where the process stands. It gives the GTF opportunities to seek input and to demonstrate its willingness to be influenced. And finally, the whole process is a "mentioning campaign" that keeps leaders and the congregation aware of the emerging structure they will be asked to approve. By getting a wide cross-section of the congregation to see the new structure as a means to achieve the congregation's mission, the process harnesses the forces of resistance and homeostasis on behalf of change.

If things go well, somebody will ask, "Didn't we already vote on this?" That's an indication that the congregation is beginning to feel that it owns the process. (Unfortunately, no amount of consultation will prevent at least one person from saying, prior to the final vote, "Nobody asked me!") To leaders, the whole process will seem repetitive, because at every step they will hear the same questions and concerns raised by a new and wider group of people. This repetition is the cost of systemic change.

The iterative process continues until the policies are complete enough to support a trial run. It is important to have top-level policies in the Governance, Management, and Oversight categories. It is not so important to create Discernment and Strategy policies; the GTF can plug existing mission statements, vision statements, and strategic plans into these categories, to be updated in the course of the annual cycle described in chapter 7. With basic criteria for oversight in place, it is safe to go ahead, delegate authority, and take the new structure on the road.

The Trial Run

In planning for the trial run, the GTF and the board will have to decide whether and how much the bylaws (or similar foundational documents) need to change. At this point, someone may suggest "suspending the bylaws." For reasons described in chapter 3, this is not ordinarily a good idea. In some polities, it may not be within the power of a local congregation to change foundational documents. Fortunately, such radical action is rarely necessary. Depending on the extent of the difference between the proposed structure and the existing one, the trial run can almost always be accomplished either with small changes to the bylaws or no changes at all.

Existing governing bodies, using their existing powers, often can enable a trial run of the proposed new structure. The details need to be worked out according to the specifics of each local situation; the general method is to ask existing governing bodies to delegate their powers in such a way as to allow the trial run to go forward. If the current board has seventy-five members, it is not necessary to abolish it for the sake of a trial run. Instead, the existing board can adopt a resolution delegating its powers to a seven-member acting board. If the bylaws list twenty-five committees, all reporting to the board, the board can delegate its oversight of the committees to the staff, with instructions to reorganize them into ministry teams. If the board chair is designated as the chief executive, the board can direct him or her to delegate that role to the head of staff. The reasoning involved[2] can be a little tricky, but it has the advantage that the existing structure is always in the wings to act as a safety net in case the experiment goes seriously awry.

It is not always possible to avoid bylaw amendments entirely, but in my opinion, it is worth the effort to keep them to a minimum. Temporary bylaw amendments—which expire unless renewed—can be useful. State law or the bylaws may require the "real" board to meet a certain number of times or to approve certain items. If so, such requirements can be met without undermining the trial run. Above all, it is a mistake to violate the bylaws. While such violations happen all the time, they are against the law and can create risks for the congregation and its leaders. It is the job of the GTF—perhaps with the assistance of ingenious legal minds—to devise a way to authorize a trial run. For the benefit of those in every congregation who need the legalities spelled out in advance of the trial run, it should also create a provisional draft of any bylaw changes that will be needed to make the new structure permanent.

In some denominations, the most fundamental rules of governance cannot be changed by the congregation at all. Substantial change is still possible, though it may take some imagination to effect, while remaining true to both the letter and the underlying values of the polity tradition.

Changes for the Board

How, exactly, life will be different during the trial run depends on the details of the proposed new structure. For the board, one starting point might be to adapt the annual board cycle described in chapter 6. At the outset there will be no pre-existing goals—or if there are, they were written under the old structure—so there can be no evaluation based on goals. As part of the overall plan for the trial run, the GTF needs to propose a way to jump-start the board's annual cycle. Perhaps the board has already adopted some goals that can be transferred to appropriate leaders according to their new responsibilities. Or the board may need to hold another retreat to develop a vision of ministry for the trial year. The timing of the trial year needs to be coordinated with events such as the annual budget, elections, denominational meetings, and clergy transitions.

The most important consideration in designing the board's work during the trial run is to make sure that board members have a good opportunity to experience the benefits of the new structure. Because the management and oversight policies are incomplete, it may be tempting to devote too much time to completing them. To yield to this temptation risks sinking the board into the very swamp of parliamentary wordsmithing from which governance change should save it. Realistically the board needs to spend some time during the trial year refining policies, but most of its time should go to creating policies on strategy and discernment. The board might identify two or three "open questions" and plan large blocks of time through the year for conversation and reflection on them. Near the midpoint of the trial year, at a leadership retreat like the one described in chapter 6, the board produces a full vision of ministry to guide goal setting for the staff, and new open questions to guide board agendas in the coming year.

Changes for the Staff

When boards turn their attention away from management to pay more attention to discernment, strategy, and oversight, the first group to feel the pinch is apt to be the staff. Congregation staff, accustomed often to a style of work that emphasizes preparation for committee meetings, may be surprised how much simpler it is to make decisions than to prepare for others to make them. Staff members may also be surprised how weighty it can feel to be responsible for outcomes.

One temple administrator put it this way: "Before, we had a problem getting anyone to provide *oneg* refreshments after service. A committee was in charge, but it didn't happen. Occasionally the board talked about it, but there was nothing they could do. Now we still have a problem getting anyone to bring *oneg* refreshments. The difference is: *I feel responsible!*"

And that is just as it should be. A board that takes responsibility for governance puts pressure on the staff (including volunteers who act as staff) to take responsibility for ministry. In congregations shifting from a board- or committee-centered model to one that entrusts the staff with a more central role in daily management, people often ask, "Who will do all of the work we now do in committees?" A simple (and sometimes disappointing) answer is that the work will be done by the same people who do it now. Congregations depend heavily on volunteers to do the work, and making staff accountable for ministry does not change that. Lines of accountability change, but groups of laypeople who teach children's classes, organize for social action, or weed the garden will look much the same before and after. The first major task for the staff is to organize existing lay leaders and volunteers as part of the staff structure. Lay members of the congregation need to continue to lead, as well as to work. The staff needs to recruit and develop not only volunteers but leaders too.

Most of the groups congregations call committees are already really teams. I recommend reserving the terms "committee" and "task force" for bodies whose job it is to help the board to make policy—either by recommending policies to the board or by designing processes to help the board make its own policies. Bodies given independent power by the bylaws, as some endowment committees are, might instead be called committees of the congregation. Groups that operate as part of the ministry staff structure are best called "teams."

Depending on the structure chosen during the preparation phase of the change process, the board may still have committees in some program areas. The children's education program might have a committee, for example, to act as a sort of mini-board for that program. If so, it is a good idea to keep the committee (which makes policy and reports to the board) conceptually separate from the ministry team (which does the work and makes decisions about how to do the work, under the direction of a staff member). This division relieves the committee of responsibility for managing the day-to-day operation of the program. As a result, its membership need not be limited to workers or other natural constituents of that area. Why should only parents have a vote on the congregation's ministry to young people or only musicians be part of the discussion about what kind of music will enhance worship?

Most of what is actually done in many congregations by committees can be carried out by "teams" or "ministries." Under the direction of the staff, following policies adopted by the board, ministry teams are freed from the implied responsibility to hold monthly meetings, keep minutes, file reports, and otherwise act like a committee. They are also free to go out of existence when their work is done, and the staff is free to create new groups to fit new tasks. Each ministry team need not be representative of the whole congregation. In fact, a team should systematically exclude anyone who does not favor accomplishing the assigned task.

When staff members are delegated full power and responsibility for ministry, their work shifts in many ways. The staff team will need patience and forbearance while its members develop new skills and habits. A budget for staff training, planning, and retreats is an important part of a successful trial run. The board will need continual reminders that its role is to tell the staff what ministry results it hopes for, not to intervene whenever the staff stumbles. A board that has been willing in the past to listen to complaints about staff members will no doubt be tested during the trial year by members hoping—often with the best intentions—to bypass the staff team by going to the board. The board needs to develop immunity to such attempts and a willingness to let the staff make its own decisions and its own mistakes. Every role will have new boundaries and new duties during the trial run. It is important to be both kind and firm in nudging people into new ways of responding to familiar situations.

Evaluation and Year Three

Toward the end of the trial year, the GTF invites the board, staff, lay leaders, and the congregation as a whole to evaluate how well the trial run addressed the concerns and achieved the goals that motivated the inquiry in the first place. The "statement of wishes" first articulated during the leadership retreat on governance is one basis for evaluation, along with other goals articulated later. As with any evaluation, achieving pre-existing goals is only one good outcome; another would be to learn to desire a different goal. It is not the main point of the evaluation to measure people's happiness. One sure result of success in any change process is that some people will become less happy. Congregations do not exist to make their members or their leaders happy; the important measure of success is whether governance helps to produce the results called for by the congregation's mission. This criterion is not easily measured, but a rough estimate is better than a thousand "metrics" that amount to nothing but opinion polls.

The GTF presents a written report of the evaluation. Because its members have an obvious stake in the success of "their" structure, the GTF should take care to summarize all feedback it receives, including criticisms. The report may recommend changes to the plan before it is made permanent; if the changes are significant, it may suggest another trial year. Otherwise, the GTF presents the proper motions to make the changes permanent. Either way, the time has come to thank the members of the GTF and to relieve them of their duties.

The role the GTF has played during the trial year is taken up by the board governance committee, whose role, as detailed in chapter 6, is to help the board monitor and improve itself. Especially during the third year, it should keep evaluation of the governance change process itself at the center of its agenda. Starting with the board's own self-critique at the end of the trial year, an effective board continually asks itself, "How well are we playing our governance roles in discernment, strategy, and oversight?"

Change can be joyous and exciting, but it is rarely easy. It takes something like four years, from the first decision to inquire into governance change, before the behavior called for by the new structure is the first idea that comes to mind. Even after that, new leaders will need to be acculturated and helped to unlearn habits they acquired in other congregations, in other nonprofits, and at work. The effort is worthwhile, though, if it creates a congregation that is better able to say what difference it means to make in people's lives, and to accomplish what it sets out to accomplish. In addition, strong governance helps congregations deal with difficulties, misbehavior, differences, and setbacks. It is to those inevitable circumstances that we turn next.

9 :: Bumps along the Road

On a warm, sunny day, you can walk outdoors with little plan or preparation. If all goes well, the stroll is easy and you return safely and on schedule. Leadership in congregations is like that too: on sunny days, almost any decision-making structure will do. But on stormy days, days when differences and tensions make life difficult, official structures for decision matter a great deal. At such times of testing, well-designed structures, policies, habits, and norms help a congregation ride the storm.

Under stress, people revert to familiar patterns of behavior. As longtime Alban Institute consultant Gil Rendle likes to say, "When a system does not know what to do, it does what it knows." Expecting challenges to be easy only makes them harder. A sense of humor, a readiness to forgive mistakes, and the expectation that change will be slow and require learning do not make the stormy days pass easily but can make them much more bearable.

It is the leaders, not the system, who must ultimately rise to times of challenge. No structure can abolish this responsibility or make it easy. It is futile, as T. S. Eliot observed, to dream "of systems so perfect that no one will need to be good."[1] But it is just as futile to imagine people so good that they have no need of systems able to respond well when they act badly. Almost any system works if it is led only by wise leaders and confronted only by routine challenges. But congregations do not always have the leaders they deserve, and even the best leaders—not to mention followers—may act less than perfectly in times of special challenge. At such times, it is important to observe established bylaws, policies, and norms instead of trying to rebuild them under pressure. So in rethinking our systems of governance, we should look ahead to some of the challenges we can expect them to encounter.

The Stress of Transition

The first major challenge after the decision to adopt a governance change may be the stress of the change itself. The first few months under a new structure almost always bring a time of stress for leaders. Even the most zealous advocates of change have days when they wish they had never heard of governance reform. Like tourists struggling to speak a foreign language, congregants and leaders feel nostalgia for familiar patterns of behavior. Staff leaders who looked forward to increased independence resist the accountability that comes with delegated power. Board members who looked forward with excitement to spending more time on discernment, strategy, and oversight find it frustrating to watch the board repeatedly slip back into making management decisions. Committee chairs who welcomed—theoretically—the goal of coordinated action long to return to their uncoordinated fiefdoms, silos, and bunkers after these are lost. A new system requires steady mental focus and continual self-correction. Sooner or later, everybody feels fatigue and longs for the relaxed routine of an unexamined, customary structure.

On one level, the solution is to suck it up and soldier on. System change is not for the faint of heart. More realistically, we all are faint of heart at times. Modest expectations and a sense of humor leaven what can be a tense and intense period. Time, the saying goes, is God's way of keeping everything from happening at once. Designing, adopting, and implementing a change of governance is no small achievement; other goals can wait. At low points in the process, it can be helpful to dust off the governance vision statement (see chapter 8) as a reminder of the reasons you embarked on this excursion in the first place.

The Board in Transition

A board used to dealing with concrete management or financial issues will at first have trouble focusing on abstract matters like mission, vision, strategy, and policy. Used to seizing on an issue and deciding it as the de facto chief executive or supreme court, the board must learn to back off from the specifics and look for the more enduring questions. Urgent issues press into the agenda at every meeting: a respected congregation member, not understanding the board's new role, comes asking for permission, approval, or money to go ahead with a project or program. Another member comes with a complaint, asking the board to put a stop to someone else's project or program. Or the challenge may come from a board member who cannot resist latching onto a small item in the treasurer's report. Instead of asking, "What should we do about this?" the board learns to ask, "What guidance might we give that will enable someone else to make decisions of this kind away from the board table?" No matter where the challenge to get off track comes from, the board must resist. The chair has a special leadership responsibility for helping the board stay on track, but he or she cannot succeed alone. Every board member needs to understand the board's new role and accept responsibility for noticing and helping to correct mistakes. Regular time for self-evaluation will help board members to share leadership.

Clarity about what the board should *not* do is only half the battle. For many boards, governance reform wipes out most of the customary agenda, leaving a vacuum that must be filled by interesting and important work. A good start is to approve a yearly rotation of major tasks and topics, as discussed in chapter 6. A clear process for adding items to the board's discussion agenda is another essential bulwark. Strong boards empower the chair or a small team to put a finger in the dike against the inflow of small items. If the board has adopted clear and complete policies on delegation, the chair or team can refer operational questions to the appropriate decision maker. Ultimately, any board member must have the right to add an item to the board agenda if he or she believes it necessary. But the board as a whole needs strong norms and boundaries to protect its precious time.

The question the board *should* consider putting on its agenda in response to operational questions is, "Do we need a policy we lack—or should we change a policy we have—in order to give adequate authority and guidance in this area?" The boundary between making policy and deciding cases is not always clear, especially to boards accustomed to deciding both. A board once boasted to me of a triumph in its delegation efforts. A teenager wanted to join an adult study group, but some members of the group objected. The teen and his parents became upset and appealed to members of staff. Inevitably, one party or the other was unhappy with the staff's decision and brought the matter to the board. Board members proudly told me, "Under the old system we would have decided yes or no. But this time we made a policy to empower the leaders of each program to decide who can participate."

With regret, I had to respond less than enthusiastically. True, the board had resisted the temptation to step into an operational decision, instead delegating a whole class of decisions to a whole class of ministry leaders. But in the process, board members defaulted on some of their own most important responsibilities. By delegating directly to so many leaders, they failed to support a unified structure for operational decision making. In effect, they bypassed the staff leadership and made themselves the direct boss of every program leader. They also failed to address—or even to identify—the underlying issue: was it the autonomy of program groups, the safety of young people, some other issue, or a combination? The board's job is to create policies that address the ethical dimensions of ministry decisions, and guide decision makers while empowering them. In delegating, the board needs to grant power, assign responsibility, and offer guidance—not an easy skill, especially for a board accustomed to making ethical decisions case by case.

By temperament, some people enjoy the concrete, immediate challenges of ministry more than the more abstract, verbal work of governance. As the board's role shifts from management to governance, some board members become less interested in the board. This diminished enthusiasm happens especially in congregations where the tacit path to board membership has run through the chairing of committees. It is important, when such people rotate off the board, to emphasize that they are not transitioning "out of leadership" but moving from leadership in governance to leadership in ministry. As the board's role changes, the staff needs to create new, high-level leadership roles within the staff structure—with appropriately grand-sounding titles!—for those former board members whose gifts will be better used there.

The Staff in Transition

In many congregations, the idea that laypeople can be asked to take high-level responsibility within the staff structure is a new one. Laypeople take high-level responsibility, of course, and cooperate with staff. But in many congregations the idea of two parallel management structures—one for volunteers, the other for paid staff—is entrenched. Both governance and ministry, as I use those terms, include paid and unpaid workers. The difference is in their functions, not their personnel. The clergy leader works closely with the governing board to interpret mission and vision. Laypeople are integrated with the staff in doing ministry—so closely integrated that I find it useful to include lay volunteers in the word "staff."

In some congregations, when the board establishes a staff-led structure for ministry decision making, some people misunderstand this action to mean that lay leaders can retire. "Disband the committees!" "No more meetings!" "Let the [paid] staff run the church!" Understandably, the people who feel the greatest stress in the early months of governance change often are the paid staff. The senior staff team has to figure out how it can be responsible for the performance of the congregation's ministry. Everything that happens needs to be connected to the staff; therefore, staff members need to network actively with programs and activities that ran themselves quite happily before. Add to that the work of writing staff-team goals, individual staff goals, and reports on progress toward achieving goals, and previously relaxed staff jobs can suddenly seem bureaucratic. It is as if each staff position had doubled in size.

The missing insight here is that governance change does not reduce the supply of potential volunteers—in fact, it can increase the supply by making volunteer roles clearer and more attractive. All the volunteers who functioned as ministry leaders in the past are still there and available, and others who were put off by the prospect of "committee work" can get excited about opportunities for ministry.

Staff Friction

For some staff teams, an additional source of stress is that latent differences sharpen into conflicts. But when the board rethinks and clarifies its role, the staff, in turn, may have to function more as a team: setting joint goals and taking responsibility for its own internal relationships, evaluation, and conflict management. When staff members work in separate "silos," they do not need to reconcile their differences of style, philosophy, and goals. But when the board improves at goal setting and evaluation, staff teamwork and supervision grow in importance, and can produce friction, as they do in other workplaces.

If the new system empowers staff to make more operational decisions, it is natural to think that the change will make staff people happy. Staff members themselves may be surprised when, in the first months under the new plan, they feel instead a crushing burden of responsibility.

To understand why they feel this way, it is important to face some uncomfortable facts about life on a congregation staff.

Most staff members work hard, and many produce clear, positive results. Each staff member attracts supporters and detractors; praising and criticizing staff performance is a popular form of entertainment in many a post-service coffee hour. But true accountability, which requires an institution-wide sense of purpose, prior understandings about goals, and a planned process of evaluation, is rare in congregations. Consequently, congregation staffs too often harbor pockets of incompetence, indolence, and—occasionally—even malfeasance. Even highly effective staff members build defensive walls around their areas of work, resisting any effort at coordination from the wider system. When the wider system's efforts at coordination are haphazard, such defensive tactics may be the best way for dedicated staff members to get their work done. But the side effects over many years can be quite serious: factions in the congregation, high staff turnover, and a strong bias against change.

Boards often contribute to poor staff performance by interpreting it as a personal failure on the part of specific staff members and by cracking down. Often the crackdown includes simplistic ways of measuring performance, punitive ways of addressing shortcomings, and the use of absurdly small amounts of money in an effort to reward performance. Such responses, while they may be based on a correct diagnosis, only make things worse. In the short term, a staff member's failure to cooperate or serve the wider mission is a personal failure—but in the long term, the failure to insist that staff members collaborate with one another and lay leaders to achieve the mission belongs to the board. A board that articulates the mission, chooses strategies, and holds regular conversations with staff leaders about how the congregation as a whole is doing will unify and direct staff energy much better than it could by punitively focusing on trivial performance metrics.

That is why it is worthwhile for boards to ask their staffs to be responsible collectively for their performance, even though the transition can be challenging. Only by designating a unified structure for staff leadership can the board escape from trying to supervise the staff, whether directly or through committees. For the same reason, wise boards expect lay leaders of ministry to work within the staff structure.

Nonetheless, any staff team—however committed it may be in principle to governance change—will have days when its members wonder why they left the comfortable chaos of the past for what feels like an unmanageable present. Every staff team will find its own way through this thicket; here are some general principles that seem to help in many situations.

Set realistic goals. In the startup phase, it is tempting to try to achieve all the benefits of a new structure at once. But staff performance issues that have languished for years do not suddenly become more urgent because someone has been made responsible for them—even if you are that someone. The same goes for weak programs, unclear policies, simmering conflicts, and neglected opportunities. Pick two or three top priorities and leave the others for another time. Most boards and staff teams find it difficult to choose a short list of priorities because that means telling important leaders and program areas that they are not—this year—a top priority. It may help to remind people that the fact that something is not a top priority does not mean it will not happen. Even the most goal-driven congregations make some of their most important progress through unplanned efforts. Serendipity and uncoordinated creativity can coexist with realistic, short lists of top goals.

Embrace the idea of lay staff. Many people's first reaction to the idea of a staff-centered structure for ministry decision making is to say, "That may be fine for bigger congregations. But we don't have anywhere nearly enough staff to make it work." If staff members try to take direct responsibility for ministry, this concern is valid. How can a staff of two or three lead programs that may involve hundreds? The answer to the seeming shortage of labor is to use the power of the men and women who have led before.

Even if your governance change has pulled the plug on a large system of committees, remember that the *people* still exist. If your building chair has traditionally run the boiler room, ask her formally to continue doing so—as an unpaid member of the staff. If you have too many ministry programs to assign each one a staff liaison, ask a lay leader to oversee a set of related programs and to attend one staff meeting a month or write a brief report. If your education committee has acted as an ersatz parent-teacher organization, appoint its former chair to organize a real one. It could meet quarterly and achieve intentionally some of what the committee achieved—building relationships, seeking input, and recruiting volunteers—without needing to spend energy looking like a committee. In many cases, traditional lay leadership jobs make more sense as staff positions anyway, and many a layperson who would never volunteer for a committee might be interested in being, say, an unpaid director of elder care.

Think of the staff as a set of concentric circles. The senior staff, consisting of two or three paid people and perhaps one super-volunteer, might meet once a week. A wider staff, including three to five more volunteers with leadership responsibilities, meets once a month. A still larger group—including everyone who leads or oversees significant activity—meets quarterly, either as a whole group or in subgroups by related subject matter. Each circle needs to connect regularly with every member of the next larger circle, parceling out liaison duties so that each leader's "span of care" is reasonable. It is not necessary to sustain a strict chain of command or rigid reporting routines; only to stay in touch sufficiently to anticipate needs, solve problems, identify vacancies, and recruit new leaders.

In addition to establishing concentric circles of staff meetings, the senior staff will want to convene ad hoc groups of leaders now and then to do specific work—for example, to create an intergenerational music program or to develop a social outreach theme. Such meetings can be initiated from above (by the head of staff or senior staff) or from below (by leaders who identify a need and call a meeting with the senior staff's support). A unified staff structure needs to be connected but does not have to be hierarchical, bureaucratic, or unreasonably labor-intensive.

It is worth remembering that though the structure has changed, the total amount of ministry and the number of available people remain the same. If the question is "How can we do this with such a small paid staff?" it may be helpful to ask, "How did we do it before (or did we?), and how can we invite the same people to take the same or more responsibility in a new structure?"

Redefine "administration" as "getting results through the efforts of others." An important limitation on the growth of many congregations is the false division between program (or "people") and administrative ("bricks, mortar, and money") staff roles. A more useful distinction is between leadership staff and individual contributors. Individual contributors apply personal skills and knowledge to lead programs, maintain buildings, play guitars, or teach children. Staff leaders recruit, train, organize, and supervise the people who do these things. In practice, most staff members—starting with the senior minister or rabbi—play both roles. Preparing a sermon is an individual contribution; so is making a pastoral call. Organizing a team for worship support or pastoral care is leadership. Many congregations understand the need for clergy and staff to spend more time equipping others to do ministry and less time doing it themselves. The next step is to develop a cadre of lay leaders whose principal job is to recruit others to do work and lead programs. This next step—developing a "middle management" of volunteers—is crucial to the growth of many congregations beyond an attendance of 250 or so.

Governance is challenging, and any change in governance creates challenges for congregation, staff, and board. The first few months of a governance transition are especially challenging. Periodic reminders of reasons for making the change in the first place help to keep leaders on track. Even more important is that leaders continue their non-leadership participation: singing in the choir, teaching Sunday school, studying the Scriptures in a small group, caring for the poor, and challenging injustice. Even if scaled back to make the time leadership requires, direct service helps to keep us centered in the congregation's higher purpose.

People Problems

The world is full of people who, for reasons of their own, behave badly. Sometimes the reasons are quite innocent: confusion, mental illness, grief, or post-traumatic stress. Other reasons are more sinister: bigotry, greed, the lust for power, or the desire to exact revenge for real or imagined injuries. Some writers about congregational conflict pay great attention to "dysfunctional" behavior, "clergy killers," and "antagonists." In my opinion, this attention is misplaced. People inclined to misbehave are distributed more or less at random through the population and can be found in every congregation. Where congregations differ is not in whether they have troublesome people or even in how often people misbehave, but in how others respond to misbehavior when it comes.

Many years ago in the church where I grew up, I saw a man approach my father after service on a Sunday when our minister was out of the pulpit. I didn't recognize the man; apparently, he was returning after a long absence and recognized my father as a fellow old-timer. After a moment's small talk, his nose wrinkled in disgust. He said, "Is that Jew still preaching here?" The question hung in the air a moment. Several people heard it, and I imagine some were struggling to frame a soft answer to defuse the situation. Not my dad. He said firmly, "There is no room in this church for that kind of talk." After another awkward silence, the man left. As far as I know, he did not return.

I would not recommend my father's bluntness to everyone. Other responses might have marked the boundaries of acceptable behavior just as well, while offering more room for the man to clean up his act and stay. But every congregation needs people—many people, not just one—who know the boundaries of acceptable behavior and feel authorized to give them voice. Such people act like antibodies in the congregational immune system, helping to sustain health and homeostasis in a world of threats. Governance can encourage healthy over unhealthy responses to misconduct and provide a means for setting limits for those who misbehave, up to and including exclusion from the congregation.

The first step in dealing with a threat—for the congregation as well as the immune system—is to identify it accurately. Objective policies, written with no specific person or situation in mind, achieve this much better than a board's deciding cases. Because of the tangled web of personal and organizational relationships, a board that first addresses misconduct in the context of a case inevitably is making moral judgments about the goodness or badness of someone who may be a friend, relative, generous donor, or active volunteer. Boards have a hard time being objective in these circumstances, and are prone to over- or underreacting on the basis of personal feelings. A healthy governance structure, like a healthy immune system, identifies and deals with threats accurately.

But note: the immune system is not a scheme for *exterminating* threats; it is the body's way of *coexisting* with them. Some parts of the immune system, like white blood cells, do kill germs, in somewhat the same way my father drove away the unlucky visitor. Just as it is possible to put too much blame on troublesome people, it is possible to give too much credit to individuals who respond helpfully to misbehavior. The immune system is a system, not an uncoordinated gang of vigilantes. White blood cells are a last resort. Most of our immunity comes from everyday, whole-body functions like firm boundaries, unimpeded circulation, body heat, and the expulsion of ingested hazardous materials. Healthy immune function is more a matter of daily routine than of emergency preparedness—though an occasional threat does keep the system toned. Without external challenges to practice on, the immune system can be compromised, so that it underreacts to big threats or overreacts to small ones.

Like all analogies, this one has its limits and its value. Misbehaving congregants and clergy are not germs, and a congregational system—Paul notwithstanding—is not exactly a body. But like a body, a congregation depends both on wise individual responses and on good organizational design. Neither good people nor good governance is enough by itself. By adopting clear policies on acceptable and unacceptable behavior, and grounding them in the congregation's ethical values, the board establishes a framework that encourages individuals to confront misbehavior informally and creates a process for dealing with it formally if need be.

Newcomers are not the only ones who misbehave in congregations. Well-established members, leaders, board members, staff and—most challenging of all—clergy misbehave as well. Sometimes misconduct—particularly in the area of finance—can be innocent, in the sense that no one is seeking personal enrichment, and so well established that no one even recognizes it. A common example is the longtime treasurer to whom everyone is understandably grateful but who fails to practice proper controls on the handling of cash, discourages a thorough audit, or protects friends who seek reimbursement for questionable or ill-documented spending.

Well-written financial policies protect the congregation's funds from misuse or misappropriation. In most cases, their more important function is to protect leaders from false accusations of misconduct. Separating the board from day-to-day financial management makes it easier for it to adopt such policies.

Misconduct in the form of boundary violations can be even harder to identify objectively, because an inappropriate relationship may come embedded in a helpful one, as when a supportive pastor becomes a sexual predator. If all misconduct were committed by irredeemably corrupt scoundrels, life would be easier. In fact, good people transgress boundaries every day and need clear policies and procedures to help them recognize the problem and address it.

Policies about misconduct must define it plainly and establish a procedure for responding. It is not possible, of course, to anticipate every kind of problem that can come up in a congregation. But using the mixing bowl analogy (see chapter 6), it is possible to define broad categories and to establish clear procedures for addressing concerns, grievances, and complaints fairly and thoroughly without burdening the board with every case.

Money Troubles

As I write, the world economy is in recession, and it appears that we may be headed for a hard time. Congregations are affected less than other charities by economic troubles—but they are not immune, especially if they depend heavily on income from investments. Local circumstances—layoffs, plant closings, or high rates of default on loans—can affect one congregation more than others. And so every congregation periodically needs to tighten its fiscal belt.

Unfortunately, in many congregations the process of decision making about money is ill-suited to the task of allocating scarce resources wisely. The implicit mental model is that the congregation's first duty is to sustain its institutional core—to maintain the building, service the debt, meet the payroll, and keep the lights on. If there is money left, we can then speak of mission, outreach, service, innovation—as if those were optional extras.

This mental map—institutional maintenance as the foundation, mission as the ground floor, innovation as a decorative filigree—does little harm so long as the supply of money grows from year to year. But in lean years, when spending needs to be trimmed back, this way of thinking can accelerate a downward spiral. Who would support a congregation that does nothing but support itself? It is relatively easy to be generous and mission-centered in times of expansion. In times of decline—or even death—it is difficult, but more important than ever, to remember that the congregation's mission is its owner.

I once consulted with a church in a magnificent Romanesque building studded with opalescent stained glass. It had a full-time minister, a full-time music director, a sixteen-voice paid choir— and in the congregation on an average Sunday, about thirty-five worshipers. This mode of operation had been financed by liberal spending from a once-large endowment and even larger withdrawals from the invisible bank account of deferred building maintenance.

Like most congregations in such circumstances, this one took pride in the heroic way it had sustained a proud tradition against long odds. But one day the treasurer reframed the situation for the members. He said, "Every day we open up our doors, we piss away fifteen hundred of God's good dollars." After a stunned silence, the discussion shifted. Instead of asking, "How can we continue to provide ourselves with a church for the longest possible time?" the group began to ask, "How can we make the most faithful use of the resources in our trust, to fulfill the true purpose of the church?"

Luckily (or providentially), the church stood next door to a museum, which purchased the building as a space to display its collection of religious art. The members decided to dissolve the congregation, leaving a substantial legacy to other churches, charities, and religious institutions. Not a perfect outcome, perhaps— what is?—but better, ethically, than simply waiting until the money was all gone.

This story is dramatic but instructive even for a congregation that is faced with trimming back by 10 or 20 percent. The easy path is to give tacit priority to existing staff positions and activities, to ignore the hidden cost of deferred building maintenance, and to cut whatever effort lacks a strong internal advocate. In many cases, it means cutting outreach giving, denominational support, and innovative projects. Or it may mean copping out of all priority decisions and enacting an across-the-board percentage cut.

In times of straitened finances, even more than in fat years, it is important that the budget process begin not with the budget from last year but with the mission. The congregation needs leaders—call them the board—capable of standing apart from the daily management of ministry. The board needs to reflect and pray about the congregation's mission and to articulate a vision for its ministry that reflects its special calling in a time of trouble. And it needs to make hard choices—sometimes choosing what is right instead of what will keep the peace.

Nothing can make budget cutting easy. But there can be some joy in it, if in the process of accepting what we can't afford to do, we reach a deeper understanding of what we must afford to do, one way or another.

— :: —

Problems are endemic to congregations, in part because people bring higher expectations and have more freedom there than they have in many other parts of their lives. It is important to remember that a flow of minor conflicts, complaints, and criticisms is part of the normal "noise level" of a congregation's life. The most helpful leadership response is often a bit less intense than the event that triggered it. By underreacting, leaders serve as step-down transformers who dampen, rather than amplify, the noise. It is worth remembering that the quiet, constant background noise is a price we pay in exchange for the creative and life-building possibilities of healthy congregations.

Organized religion is a paradox worth puzzling over, a polarity worth managing, and an oxymoron worthy of a laugh. Congregations can infuriate, amuse, and outrage us—and they can protect the vulnerable, inspire the cynical, and heal the sin-sick soul. Leaders who know how to walk the fuzzy line each day between creative anarchy and excessive order help to transform lives for the better. Sometimes, in the process, their own lives are transformed as well.

Notes

Chapter 1 :: Organized Religion

1. Not all congregations are incorporated; most begin life as unincorporated associations. It is easy to confuse the various aspects of "nonprofit status," which include incorporation, exemption from federal and state income tax, and exemption from various property and sales taxes. All of these are technically separate, though most congregations have them all. The IRS does not distinguish incorporated and unincorporated associations when determining tax exemption.

Until recently, the constitutions of Virginia and West Virginia actually prohibited congregations from incorporating. This policy dates from the eighteenth and early nineteenth centuries, when corporate status was a special privilege usually granted by vote of the state legislature. In this context, James Madison and others viewed the granting of corporate status to a church as an establishment of religion, contrary to the spirit of religious freedom. Today incorporation is generally available to qualified applicants; most congregations avail themselves of it to limit the personal liability of members and officers, to qualify for grants, and to simplify owning property, borrowing money, and many other business matters. In 2002, a federal district court held Virginia's policy, along with several other special limitations on churches, unconstitutional. Although the U.S. Supreme Court has not ruled on the question, it seems likely that it would extend the option of incorporating to congregations in the Virginias. See H. Robert Showers,

"Incorporation of Churches in Virginia: A New Day and Law," a paper published on the website of First Baptist Church, Leesburg, Virginia, *http://www.fbcwoodbridge.org.*

2. The words "power" and "authority" overlap in meaning. "Power," as I use the word, means the ability to make things happen by legal right or other compulsion. The power of attorney, the powers of Congress, and the power that corrupts (or corrupts absolutely) are examples of the kind of power I mean. "Authority" is legitimate power. We appeal to authority to justify our power, and do things "by the authority" of others. When Jesus interpreted the Law, he spoke "as one with authority." In using the words this way, I am walking roughly in parallel with Max Weber's use of the German terms *Macht* and *legitime Herrschaft* (legitimate control), which are traditionally translated "power" and "authority." See Max Weber, *Theory of Social and Economic Organization* (New York: Free Press, 1964), 152–53. In English, the word "authority" comes from the same root as "author," suggesting that authority might carry with it some creative license. When a board charges someone with fulfilling some aspect of the mission without specifying exactly how it should be done, it delegates authority.

3. Mark Chaves, *Congregations in America* (Cambridge: Harvard University Press, 2004), table on p. 19. Chaves finds that the median American congregation has seventy-five "regularly participating individuals," of whom fifty are adults.

4. "Guiding Principles for a Free Faith," in James Luther Adams, *On Being Human Religiously: Selected Essays in Religion and Society*, ed. Max L. Stackhouse (Boston: Skinner House Books, 1976), 17.

Chapter 2 :: Governance and Ministry in Interesting Times

1. James Hudnut-Beumler, *In Pursuit of the Almighty's Dollar: A History of Money and American Protestantism* (Chapel Hill: University of North Carolina Press, 2007), 132–41.

2. "Attacks Women Drinkers: Ohio Prohibition Chairman Thinks Woman Suffrage Aids Liquor Traffic," *New York Times*, July 14, 1908, 2.

3. D. Michael Lindsay and George Gallup Jr., *Surveying the Religious Landscape: Trends in U.S. Beliefs* (Harrisburg, Pa.: Morehouse Group, 2000), 7.

4. Will Herberg, *Protestant Catholic Jew: An Essay in American Religious Sociology* (New York: Doubleday & Co., 1955).

5. Pew Forum on Religion & Public Life, *U.S. Religious Landscape Survey* (Washington: Pew Research Center, 2008), *http://religions.pewforum.org/reports*; Robert C. Fuller, *Spiritual, but Not Religious: Understanding Unchurched America* (New York: Oxford University Press, USA, 2001).

6. Thomas A. Gerace, "Harvard Business School Case Study 9–396–051, Encyclopaedia Britannica," rev. 1997, *http://harvardbusinessline.hbsp.harvard.edu*.

7. John L. Ronsvalle and Sylvia Ronsvalle, *The State of Church Giving through 2005: Abolition of the Institutional Enslavement of Overseas Missions* (Urbana, Ill.: Empty Tomb, 2007), 17.

Chapter 3 ∷ How Congregations Organize

1. R. Stephen Warner, "The Place of the Congregation in the Contemporary American Religious Configuration," in *American Congregations, Volume 2: New Perspectives in the Study of Congregations*, ed. James P. Wind and James W. Lewis (Chicago: University of Chicago Press, 1998), 54–99.

2. American National Red Cross, *American Red Cross Governance for the 21st Century: A Report to the Board of Governors* (Washington: American National Red Cross, October 2006).

3. David McCullough, *1776* (New York: Simon & Schuster, 2005).

4. William M. Easum and Thomas G. Bandy, *Growing Spiritual Redwoods* (Nashville: Abingdon, 1997); Richard Warren, *The Pur-*

pose Driven Church: Growth without Compromising Your Message and Mission (Grand Rapids: Zondervan, 1995).

5. Joy Skjegstad, *Starting a Nonprofit at Your Church* (Herndon, Va.: Alban Institute, 2002), includes a good discussion of the pros and cons of establishing a separate board for subsidiary enterprises (1–17).

6. Richard R. Hammar, *Pastor, Church and Law*, 4 vols., 4th ed. (Carol Stream, Ill.: Christian Ministry Resources, 2000), 276.

Chapter 4 :: A Map for Thinking about Congregations

1. The phrase "holy conversation" comes from a book that has helped shape my thinking in many ways, as have its authors: Gil Rendle and Alice Mann, *Holy Conversations: Strategic Planning as a Spiritual Practice for Congregations* (Herndon, Va.: Alban Institute, 2003).

2. This is as good a place as any to acknowledge a huge debt to Richard Chait, William P. Ryan, and Barbara E. Taylor. They identify three modes of board governance—fiduciary, strategic, and generative—that correspond roughly to my categories of oversight, strategy, and discernment. See *Governance as Leadership: Reframing the Work of Nonprofit Boards* (Hoboken, N.J.: John Wiley & Sons, 2005).

Chapter 5 :: The Job of the Board

1. Edward Le Roy Long, *Patterns of Polity: Varieties of Church Governance* (Cleveland: Pilgrim Press, 2001), 64.

2. For the technical-minded: a legal trust creates three roles: a trustor, also known as settler or donor; a trustee; and a beneficiary. More than one person or institution can play each role, and sometimes the same party plays two roles. In a typical trust, the trustor places assets into the trust, so that the trustee can control them for the good of the beneficiary. The trust document tells the

trustee how trust resources must be managed and the purposes for which they can be disbursed. The trustee is in a fiduciary relation to both trustor and beneficiary; in fact, the duties of trustees have become an influential legal model for the duties of all other fiduciaries. Stockholders, as owners of a business corporation, occupy a position analogous to a trustor who is also the beneficiary; stockholders put up the initial money and have a right to benefit if the enterprise succeeds. The board of directors stands in a fiduciary relationship to stockholders. In a nonprofit corporation, donors are like stockholders in that they put up the initial cash, but because their contribution is a gift, they do not have a right to benefit from it, either by a payout from corporate funds or by retaining control of the organization, so the word "owner" does not fit them very well. Members, too, if a nonprofit has them, are forbidden to benefit personally from its operation. While the board and congregation have the *legal* right to control the congregation, it is the mission that has the *moral* right both to control the congregation's actions and to benefit from them. Mission is to a congregation what stockholders are to a business corporation.

3. Peter F. Drucker, *Managing the Non-Profit Organization: Practices and Principles* (New York: HarperCollins, 1990), xiv.

4. A superb guide to congregational strategic planning is Rendle and Mann, *Holy Conversations*.

5. *Holy Conversations*, xiv.

Chapter 6 :: Productive Board Meetings

1. C. Northcote Parkinson, *Parkinson's Law: And Other Studies in Administration* (New York: Ballantine Books, 1964), 40.

2. I have adapted Carver's ideas freely. His ideas about policies can be found in John Carver, *Boards that Make a Difference: A New Design for Leadership in Nonprofit and Public Organizations*, 3rd ed. (San Francisco: Jossey-Bass, 2006), 21–49; and John Carver and Miriam Mayhew Carver, *Reinventing Your Board: A Step-by-*

Step Guide to Implementing Policy Governance, rev. ed. (San Francisco: John Wiley & Sons, 2006), 17–37.

3. Henry M. Robert, *Robert's Rules of Order*, 1893 edition, ed. Rachel Vixman (New York: Pyramid, 1976); Henry M. Robert, *Robert's Rules of Order Revised for Deliberative Assemblies* (Chicago: Scott, Foresman, 1915), available online (*http://www.bartleby.com/176/*); Henry M. Robert et al., *Robert's Rules of Order: Newly Revised*, 10th ed. (Cambridge, Mass.: Da Capo Press, 2000).

4. These provisions can be found in Section 48 of any recent *Robert's*. The original and 1915 versions barely mention boards at all.

5. U.S. Army Corps of Engineers, "Office of History Vignette No. 38: Did You Know? An Army Engineer Brought Order to Church Meetings and Revolutionized Parliamentary Procedure?" (*http://www.hq.usace.army.mil/History/Vignettes/Vignette_38.htm*).

6. Notably Alice Sturgis, *The Standard Code of Parliamentary Procedure*, 4th ed. (New York: McGraw-Hill, 1993).

7. "Calling the question" is a corrupt form of the *Robert's* motion to "Put the Previous Question," which is not debatable and requires a two-thirds vote, because it has the effect of limiting the normal right of members to debate. In a large meeting, the chairperson's proper response, since hardly anyone knows what the previous question is, is to rephrase it: "The member has moved to cut off debate and vote immediately. Is there a second? Since there are members who wish to speak, cutting off debate requires a two-thirds vote. Will those in favor say 'aye.' Those opposed, 'no.'" In a board of a dozen or fewer members, the chairperson's proper response (under *Robert's*) is to rule the motion out of order because it is inappropriate for a small body.

8. Outi Flynn, *Meet Smarter: A Guide to Better Nonprofit Board Meetings* (Washington, D.C.: Boardsource, 2004), 17–18.

9. The stock exchange rules are posted at *http://www.sec.gov/rules/sro/34-48745.htm*.

10. The provisions of Sarbanes-Oxley that do apply to non-profits are the ones requiring written policies on whistleblower protection and destruction of old documents. BoardSource, "The Sarbanes-Oxley Act and Implications for Nonprofit Organizations," *http://www.boardsource.org*, 9–10.

11. BoardSource, "Executive Sessions: How to Use Them Regularly and Wisely," *http://www.boardsource.org*.

12. Marla J. Bobowick, Sandra Hughes, and Berit M. Lakey, *Transforming Board Structure: Strategies for Committees and Task Forces* (Washington, D.C.: BoardSource, 2001), 26–31.

Chapter 7 ∷ Lay and Clergy Partnership

1. Readers looking for a guide to congregational administration might wish to consult Gilbert R. Rendle and Susan Beaumont, *When Moses Meets Aaron: Staffing and Supervision in Large Congregations* (Herndon, Va.: Alban Institute, 2007); and Robert F. Leventhal, *Stepping Forward: Synagogue Visioning and Planning* (Herndon, Va.: Alban Institute, 2007).

2. Carver, *Boards that Make a Difference*, 72.

3. A helpful guide to evaluation of both clergy and others is Jill M. Hudson, *When Better Isn't Enough: Evaluation Tools for the 21st-Century Church* (Herndon, Va.: Alban Institute, 2004).

Chapter 8 ∷ Exploring Governance Change

1. Did you hear the one about the computer programmer who drowned in the shower? He read the instructions on the shampoo bottle: "Lather, rinse, repeat."

2. Theologically trained readers will recognize the type of reasoning I'm talking about as "casuistry," a time-honored mode of thinking that begins with a desired conclusion and works backward to the premises. Computer-savvy readers will recognize the

trial run as a "virtual machine" like the software that fools Windows programs into running on a Mac.

Chapter 9 :: Bumps along the Road

1. T. S. Eliot, "Choruses from the Rock," *Collected Poems, 1909–1962* (New York: Harcourt Brace Jovanovich, 1991), 158.

Bibliography

American National Red Cross. *American Red Cross Governance for the 21st Century: A Report to the Board of Governors.* Washington: American National Red Cross, October 2006.

Anheier, Helmut. *Nonprofit Organizations: Theory, Management, Policy*, 1st ed. London and New York: Routledge, 2005.

Blanchard, Ken, Patricia Zigarmi, and Drea Zigarmi. *Leadership and the One Minute Manager: Increasing Effectiveness through Situational Leadership*, 1st ed. New York: William Morrow, 1985.

Blanchard, Kenneth H., and Spencer Johnson. *The One Minute Manager*, rev. ed. New York: HarperCollins Business, 2000.

BoardSource. *Exceptional Board Practices: The Source in Action.* Washington: BoardSource, 2008.

Bobowick, Marla J., Sandra Hughes, and Berit M. Lakey. *Transforming Board Structure: Strategies for Committees and Task Forces.* Washington: BoardSource, 2001.

Busby, Dan. *Church and Nonprofit Tax and Financial Guide.* Grand Rapids: Zondervan, 2007.

Butler, Lawrence. *The Nonprofit Dashboard: A Tool for Tracking Progress.* Washington: BoardSource, 2007.

Carver, John. *Boards that Make a Difference: A New Design for Leadership in Nonprofit and Public Organizations*, 3rd ed. San Francisco: Jossey-Bass, 2006.

Carver, John, and Miriam Mayhew Carver. *Reinventing Your Board: A Step-by-Step Guide to Implementing Policy Governance*, rev. ed. San Francisco: John Wiley & Sons, 2006.

Chaffee, Paul. *Accountable Leadership: A Resource Guide for Sustaining Legal, Financial, and Ethical Integrity in Today's Congregations,* 1st ed. San Francisco: Jossey-Bass, 1997.

Chait, Richard, William P. Ryan, and Barbara E. Taylor. *Governance as Leadership: Reframing the Work of Nonprofit Boards.* Hoboken, N.J.: John Wiley & Sons, 2005.

Chaves, Mark. *Congregations in America.* Cambridge, Mass.: Harvard University Press, 2004.

Cladis, George. *Leading the Team-Based Church: How Pastors and Church Staffs Can Grow Together into a Powerful Fellowship of Leaders.* A Leadership Network Publication, 1st ed. San Francisco: Jossey-Bass, 1999.

Cobble, James F., Jr., Richard R. Hammar, and Steven W. Klipowicz. *Reducing the Risk II: Making Your Church Safe from Child Sexual Abuse.* Carol Stream, Ill.: Church Law and Tax Report, 2003.

Drucker, Peter F. *Managing the Non-Profit Organization: Practices and Principles.* New York: HarperCollins, 1990.

Fletcher, Kathleen. *The Policy Sampler: A Resource for Nonprofit Boards.* Washington: BoardSource, 2000.

Flynn, Outi. *Meet Smarter: A Guide to Better Nonprofit Board Meetings.* Washington: BoardSource, 2004.

Fremont-Smith, Marion R. *Governing Nonprofit Organizations: Federal and State Law and Regulation.* Cambridge, Mass.: Belknap Press of Harvard University Press, 2004.

Hall, P. D. *A History of Nonprofit Boards in the United States.* BoardSource e-book series. Washington: BoardSource, 2003. www.boardsource.org.

Hammar, Richard. *2008 Church and Clergy Tax Guide.* Carol Stream, Ill.: Christianity Today, 2007.

——— *Pastor, Church and Law.* 4 vols., 4th ed. Carol Stream, Ill.: Christian Ministry Resources, 2007.

Hudson, Jill M. *When Better Isn't Enough: Evaluation Tools for the 21st-Century Church.* Bethesda, Md.: Alban Institute, 2004.

Kurtz, Daniel L., and Sarah E. Paul. *Managing Conflicts of Interest: A Primer for Nonprofit Boards.* Washington: BoardSource, 2006.

Lang, Andrew S. *Financial Responsibilities of Nonprofit Boards*, 2nd ed. Washington: BoardSource, 2003.

Leventhal, Robert. *Byachad: Synagogue Board Development.* Herndon, Va.: Alban Institute, 2007.

Long, Edward Le Roy. *Patterns of Polity: Varieties of Church Governance.* Cleveland: Pilgrim Press, 2001.

Mann, Alice. *Raising the Roof: The Pastoral-to-Program Size Transition.* Bethesda, Md.: Alban Institute, 2001.

———. *The In-Between Church: Navigating Size Transitions in Congregations.* Bethesda, Md.: Alban Institute, 1998.

Ober Kaler, Attorneys at Law. *The Nonprofit Legal Landscape.* Washington: BoardSource, 2005.

Olsen, Charles M. *Transforming Church Boards into Communities of Spiritual Leaders.* Washington: Alban Institute, 1995.

Phillips, Roy D. *Letting Go: Transforming Congregations for Ministry.* Bethesda, Md.: Alban Institute, 1999.

Rendle, Gil, and Alice Mann. *Holy Conversations: Strategic Planning as a Spiritual Practice for Congregations.* Bethesda, Md.: Alban Institute, 2003.

Rendle, Gilbert R. *Behavioral Covenants in Congregations: A Handbook for Honoring Differences.* Bethesda, Md.: Alban Institute, 1999.

Rendle, Gilbert R., and Susan Beaumont. *When Moses Meets Aaron: Staffing and Supervision in Large Congregations.* Herndon, Va.: Alban Institute, 2007.

Robert, Henry M., William J. Evans, Daniel H. Honemann, Thomas J. Balch, and Sarah Corbin Robert. *Robert's Rules of Order: Newly Revised*, 10th ed. Cambridge, Mass.: Da Capo Press, 2000.

Skjegstad, Joy. *Starting a Nonprofit at Your Church.* Herndon, Va.: Alban Institute, 2002.

Steinke, Peter L. *Healthy Congregations: A Systems Approach*, 2nd ed. Herndon, Va.: Alban Institute, 2006.

———. *How Your Church Family Works: Understanding Congregations as Emotional Systems.* Herndon, Va.: Alban Institute, 2006.

Wind, James P., and James Welborn Lewis. *American Congregations*, 2 vols. Chicago: University of Chicago Press, 1994.

Board Time Analysis

This exercise will help your board to focus critically on how it uses its time, and it may motivate board members to consider a change of practice.

Preparation. Choose three sets of board minutes that are at least a year old but less than two years old. Choose minutes old enough to reduce the temptation to rehash past agenda items but new enough to reflect current board practice. Make one copy of each set of board minutes. If your board has more than fifteen members, make enough additional copies that you have one for every four to six board members—but do not use more than three different sets of minutes.

Choose a meeting room with space for the board members to move their chairs and work comfortably in small groups. Preferably the space should *not* be the one where the board usually meets. Set up an easel with newsprint and a supply of markers with ink in them (Make sure to check for ink!). Obtain a whiteboard, chalkboard, or two easels with newsprint that can be used as one large drawing space.

Recruit a person or a small committee to record the results of this exercise and to turn them into policy about the board's agenda for action at the next official board meeting.

Process. On the whiteboard, draw two concentric circles. Label the inmost circle CORE BOARD ROLES. Label the larger circle BOARD WORK. Label the part of the sheet that is outside both circles NON-BOARD WORK.

Figure A.1

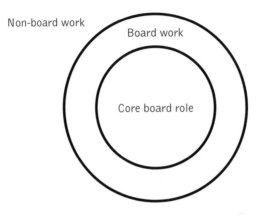

Explain that governing boards have some *core* functions—jobs that only the board can do. Boards also spend time on *board work* that may be appropriate for the board but that could be done by others. Unfortunately, boards sometimes spend time doing things it would be better for them not to do: *non-board work.*

Ask, "What are our core functions? What are the jobs only the board can do?" Possible answers include *mission, hiring staff, the budget,* or *setting direction.* Don't worry at this point about whether the responses are consistent or correct. Just write them down in the inner circle.

Now ask, "What are some examples of work a board should *not* do?" Likely responses include *micromanaging, complaining, socializing,* and *redoing committee work.* Write all responses on the right side of the board.

Finally, point to the ring labeled "board work" and ask, "What are some jobs that are appropriate for a board to do that we could delegate if we chose to?" Often at this point someone will suggest that items from the first two lists belong in this category. Acknowledge that there may be different ideas in the room about what a board should do. When someone suggests that an item should fall into a different category, draw an arrow from the part of the diagram where that item appears to the newly suggested location.

Allow a little time for discussion. Encourage a spirit of open inquiry and mutual interest, and discourage criticism or a rush to premature consensus.

Say, "We've taken a look at some of our ideas about what boards ought to do. Now we're going to take a look at what we actually do." Hand out copies of the Board Time Analysis Form on page 216, and spend a few minutes going over the categories. "Responding to requests for permission or approval" includes any discussion about a board action that would control a one-time event. Approving even a large one-time event like a building program, staff hire, or capital campaign falls into this category and is quite different from adopting a policy that will govern a series of similar decisions in the future. "Carrying out *scheduled* staff evaluation" is not the same as voicing ad-hoc criticisms or complaints. "Choosing priorities for coming years" includes only priorities that affect years starting after today. "Learning together" might mean hearing an outside speaker, reading a book together, or studying demographic data about the wider community.

If some categories are ambiguous in your situation, agree on a definition or rewording you will use for this exercise. If your board spends substantial time on something that does not seem to fit into any of the given categories, add your own.

Divide the board into working groups of four to six. Give each working group one set of the minutes you collected (see the preparation section above). If your board is larger than eighteen members, you may need to give copies of the same minutes to more than one working group.

Ask each working group to look at the minutes together and estimate how much time was spent at the meeting on each of the types of activity listed on the form. Probably the minutes will not give this information directly, so to complete the sheet the working groups may need to rely on their memories of the meeting, their experience of how long it typically takes for the board to deal with certain types of questions, or simple guesswork. Encourage each group to see if its members can agree on their estimates, and to fill out the form for the whole group. Getting exact results is less important than giving the board a chance to think together about how it spends its time. Allow about fifteen minutes for this part of the exercise.

Re-gather the group. Create a newsprint sheet with a shortened version of the categories from the Board Time Analysis Form (see page 216), like this:

Figure A.3

Category	Percentage
Prayer, ritual, study	
Minutes, reports	
Permission, approval	
Scheduled evaluation	
Written policies	
Priorities	
Learning together	
Changes in our ministry or operation	

Say, "Let's hear from one of the groups about 'Prayer, ritual, and study.' What percentage did you assign to that one?" After someone answers, ask, "Did any group give a lower score? How about higher?" When you've heard the range (for example, 10 to 15 percent), write the range in the right-hand column of the newsprint. Repeat for each category. If you like, you might ask the whole board to estimate the percentage of its time it spends on each category on a year-round basis.

Compare your self-ratings with the results of the "Board Work/ Non-Board Work" exercise. Many boards will find that they spend a great deal of time hearing reports and updates, giving incremental approvals for ongoing work, and discussing the crisis of the moment. Too often they spend little or no time on any of the other items. Allocating more time for the others would produce longer-lasting results for the congregation.

To wind up this exercise, turn to a new piece of newsprint and ask, "How would we like to change the way we use our time in the future?" Write down the answers that seem to have consensus support.

Then say, "Looking at this list, what instructions might we want to give to the people who prepare our agenda?" Some ideas for instructions follow:

- Plan a fifteen-minute conversation about our congregation's mission that will follow devotions at the beginning of each meeting.
- Require all reports to be sent in writing to board members in advance of meetings, with board action items clearly identified at the top of each report. Do not use meeting time for reports.
- Avoid presenting the board with one-time action items, and reframe all issues as ongoing policy proposals whenever possible.

When all proposals have been listed, take a straw poll on each, and ask those who have volunteered to carry the results of this exercise forward if they have any questions they need answered to carry out their charge.

Often this exercise produces agreement on a few improvements to the board's use of time. It may also lead to a more comprehensive program of study and reform using ideas found elsewhere in this book.

Figure A.2

BOARD TIME ANALYSIS FORM

Time categories	Time in minutes	Percent
Prayer, meditation, ritual, personal check-in, and study of religious texts		
Presenting and discussing minutes, reports, and financial statements		
Responding to requests for permission or approval		
Carrying out scheduled evaluation of clergy, staff, programs, or projects		
Discussing additions or amendments to our written policies		
Choosing financial, program, and staffing priorities for coming years		
Learning together about new ideas and information		
Considering significant changes in the congregation's future ministry or mode of operation		
Other:		
Other:		
Other:		
TOTALS		100%

Policy Book Outline

No board should adopt a set of boilerplate policies. Congregations are too varied and their organizational norms too closely intertwined with their core values for generic policies to fit. An even more important reason is that making policy is the heart of the board's work. Strong boards do not delegate policy making even to their own committees. If a policy is too trivial to merit the board's attention, it should be made by staff. If a policy is too technical for the board to understand, the board should educate itself so that it can carry out its own responsibilities. A committee might facilitate a good board conversation by developing a list of key questions or a set of policy alternatives. But in the end, the board itself will be responsible for its policies and should write— not rubberstamp—them.

The outline shown in figure B.1 (Board Policy Book) includes many of the policy topics congregational boards may need to cover. The first heading, "Governance," includes the board's policies for its own self-management. The other four section headings correspond to the four categories of policy defined in chapter 5—discernment, strategy, management, and oversight. In some cases, I will offer one or more examples based on the work of other congregations. Every congregation will need many policies in addition to those shown here.

If you are writing policies from scratch, I suggest the sequence described in chapter 8. Begin with the introductory "philosophy of governance" statement, and get your board to bless it before

Figure B.1

BOARD POLICY BOOK

GOVERNANCE

Philosophy of governance

Board covenant

Board self-government
- Board agenda
- Board committees
- Conflicts of interest
- Discipline and removal of board members

DISCERNMENT

Mission statement
- Who are we?
- What difference do we make, and for whom?

Core values
- What principles do we intend to observe, no matter what?

Open questions
- What are the unanswered questions about our mission that we will reflect upon in the coming year?

STRATEGY

Strategic plan
- What major choices have we made about how we will fulfill our mission?
- Program development plan
- Membership development plan
- Capital plan
- Staffing plan

Vision of ministry
- In what new and different ways will we transform lives in the next 3-5 years?
- Program development goals
- Membership development goals
- Capital budget
- Operating budget

MANAGEMENT

Delegation to the staff
- Global delegation
- Staff structure

Delegation to others

Care for people
- Health & safety
- Nondiscrimination
- Universal access

Care for staff
- Compensation & benefits
- Creating & filling staff positions
- Discipline and discharge of staff
- Whistle-blower protection
- Grievances
- Personnel manual

Care for resources
- Financial controls
- Insurance
- Capital reserves and endowments
- Document retention

Powers reserved to the board

OVERSIGHT

Monitoring
- Financial reports
- Staff reports
- Board inquiries
- Financial audit

Evaluation
- Program evaluation
- Board and head of staff evaluation
- Staff evaluations
- Clergy leader performance review

you spend time building a sand castle that will get kicked down as soon as it is finished. Second, write the policies on management. Once you're clear who will be responsible for daily management, you're ready for the third step, policies on oversight. Once the policies on philosophy, delegation, and oversight have been completed and approved, the congregation can proceed with a trial run of the new system, leaving the policies on discernment and strategy to emerge from the board's ongoing process of goal setting and evaluation.

If a board already has adopted some policies, it can be tempting simply to plug them into the appropriate sections. Remember, though, that a shift in the board's role may mean that policies it has adopted in the past may not be appropriate in the future. John Carver's "mixing bowl" principle, described in chapter 6, can be helpful: always write the largest, most general policies in each subject area first. It may seem silly to write basic principles (such as "The business manager shall safeguard the congregation's funds"). But it is a good discipline to start by stating the overall intent before spelling out details ("Checks over $5,000 shall require two signatures"). At each level, the board should ask itself, "Can we stop here? Have we said enough that we are ready to trust those to whom we have delegated operational authority to decide cases guided by what we have written, or do we really need to pin it down some more?" Most boards that adopt this step-by-step procedure find that they stop sooner than they thought they would. Smaller policies can be handed over to the staff, which may wish to publish its own book of staff policies. (Sometimes staff policies are called "procedures" to distinguish them from board policies, and to emphasize that board policies take precedence.)

Governance

Governance is the board's work, to be accomplished not in isolation but in "holy conversation" among board members, clergy, staff, and congregation. State law and denominational polity lay out the essential scope and limits of the board's powers. Policies on governance do not duplicate or modify those higher laws, but announce how the board intends to play its role.

Philosophy of Governance

A statement of governance philosophy is a good place to begin. It is useful both as an early step in the governance change process described in chapter 8, and as a resource for orienting new board members to their work.

EXAMPLE

The congregation elects a board to function as its governing body and a minister to serve as its spiritual, programmatic, and administrative leader. The intended style of leadership shall be consultative, collegial, and inclusive. We shall strive to delegate authority to leaders in proportion to their responsibilities. We expect all leaders to practice open decision making, healthy conflict management, and mutual support in their respective roles.

EXAMPLE

Governance is a collective, democratic process that produces lasting policies designed to direct many individual decisions. It is best accomplished through democratic or representative bodies, including congregational meetings, the board of trustees, and board working groups. The board of trustees, under the leadership of the president, is responsible for leading the governance of the church. As much as possible, the board shall delegate management decision making and devote its own attention to discernment, strategy, and oversight.

EXAMPLE

The board's focus shall be on the long-term mission and well-being of the congregation, not on administrative detail. It shall respect the distinction between board governance and ministry, and shall avoid when possible making decisions that address only a single situation.

The board intends to govern primarily by

- Discerning and articulating the congregation's mission and vision of ministry,
- Setting goals and making strategic choices,
- Creating written policies to guide the congregation's ministry, and
- Monitoring and evaluating the congregation's leadership, including itself.

Board Covenant

The board covenant spells out what the board expects of its members and the practices and spiritual disciplines it means to follow as a body. Every board needs expectations about preparation, attendance, participation, and conflict management; and agreement on the basic fiduciary duties of care, loyalty, and obedience. Beyond those basics, covenant language can vary as much as congregations and their faith traditions vary, so that understandings among board members can be brought under the watching eye of what each congregation holds most sacred.

EXAMPLE

Board members shall attend all duly called board meetings and actively participate in carrying out the mission of the board. Members who for any reason are unable to fulfill their responsibilities for a period of six months or more or who, because of changed circumstances, come to anticipate that they shall be unable to fulfill their responsibilities for an extended period shall be expected to submit their resignations. The secretary of each board shall direct a letter to any board member who fails to attend any meeting of the board over a period of six months, calling attention to this provision.

EXAMPLE

We, the board of the ——— Congregation, covenant to serve the congregation's mission as well as the members of the congregation.

We shall create an atmosphere of compassionate candor by presuming good faith, actively listening, not interrupting, and staying in relationship with one another, even in conflict. We shall respect our time together by honoring our commitments, being prepared for meetings, and handling non-meeting business outside of board meetings. We shall focus on policy, not micromanagement. We shall stand by our group decisions and speak with one voice.

We shall continually learn as a board and deepen our sense of spirituality.

EXAMPLE (ST. TIMOTHY'S EPISCOPAL CHURCH, HERNDON, VA)

Vestry meetings are the fourth Monday of each month. We begin promptly at 7:30 p.m.

Clergy and wardens develop the agenda prior to the meeting. Requests to be on the agenda should be made no later than the week before. Agendas and previous minutes shall be placed in mailboxes or e-mailed before the vestry meeting.

Additions to the agenda on the night of the meeting should be made for items requiring immediate attention only. Ordinarily, nothing is brought before the vestry that has not been thoroughly discussed by a ministry group or task force, with a recommendation to the vestry for action.

Attendance at all vestry meetings is very important. If a member must be late or absent, that vestry member is expected to notify the rector or the senior warden prior to the meeting. If a vestry member misses more than three meetings in a calendar year, he/she may be replaced by the alternate.

Vestry members do not represent any group within the parish. The vestry is charged with responsibility for the money and property of the church. We therefore work for the good of the whole parish.

The work of the vestry occasionally calls for a committee or task force comprised of members of the vestry. Members are expected to assume their fair share of this special work.

As spiritual leaders, vestry members also serve the parish by our attendance and participation in parish functions: e.g., special congregational meetings, special worship services, etc.

Each vestry member (except the senior warden, treasurer, and registrar) is a liaison with a standing ministry of the church. The liaison maintains close contact with the chairperson and ministry members. Each liaison reports to the vestry on the work of the ministry to which they are liaison.

Vestry members attend a weekend retreat every year in January at the church's expense.

EXAMPLE (UNION FOR REFORM JUDAISM)

Brit Avodah (covenant of service). Do what is right and good in the sight of the Eternal (Deuteronomy 6:18).

It is the responsibility of board members of congregations of the Union for Reform Judaism (URJ) to ensure that the synagogue is an ethical stronghold in all its pursuits and dealings. Board members should be guided by *kedushah* (holiness) in promoting the synagogue's mission of sustaining Judaism. Their role is that of "managing the sacred," by bringing vision, wisdom, and dedication to their duties. Board members enter into a *brit kodesh* (sacred covenant). In doing so, they shall adhere to the following principles:

Congregational expectations. Board members are expected to:

- Set the synagogue's mission and purpose, goals, and strategic direction and implement these through congregational programs and services, working closely with clergy and staff (in those congregations with clergy and staff).
- Be actively involved in the organizational and communal life of the synagogue by frequently attending worship services, board and committee meetings, along with congregational events.
- Be familiar with the congregation's bylaws, policies, and traditions, as well as its financial affairs.
- Ensure sound financial and organizational structure and procedures, and exercise fiduciary oversight.
- Be responsive to the congregation's members, providing support and listening to their needs.
- Strengthen the congregation's role in the local community, relationship to the URJ and to Israel.

Personal expectations. Board members should expect to:

- Gain spiritual and personal growth through prayer and Jewish study.
- Set an example through personal commitment and actions, serving as role models.
- Use their skills to participate fully and thoughtfully in synagogue governance.
- Work collaboratively with the clergy, professional staff (in those congregations with clergy and staff), and members of the congregation.
- Act as advocates and positive spokespersons for the synagogue, its personnel, programs, and policies.
- Embrace *tzedakah* (righteous action) by financially supporting their synagogue to the best of their ability.
- Be part of the creative process of sustaining Jews and Judaism *l'dor v'dor* (from generation to generation).
- Board members can expect to be appropriately recognized for their efforts.

Accountability. Board members are accountable for:

- Decision making based upon Jewish values such as fairness, *derech eretz*, mutual respect, sensitivity, and openness.
- Acting with personal honesty and integrity, including avoiding personal gain and conflict of interest.
- Providing oversight and fiscal responsibility so that resources are used effectively.
- Engaging in regular evaluation of policies, programs, procedures, and personnel.
- Preserving the dignity of the synagogue, each of its members and those who serve it.
- Supporting both positively and Jewishly the daily work of the clergy and professional staff (in congregations with clergy and professional staff).
- Creating a safe and welcoming environment, built on trust, for all congregants and employees (where there are employees).

Communication and confidentiality. Board members are responsible for:

- Ensuring that matters requiring confidentiality are unequivocally respected.
- Upholding to the highest standards the laws of *la-shon harah* (idle gossip or slanderous talk).
- Respecting the privacy of deliberations and discussions that take place within meetings.
- Communicating openly and truthfully with fellow lay leaders, clergy, professional staff, and congregants.
- Ensuring that criticism of policy, positions, programs, or individuals is expressed constructively and addressed to the appropriate party.
- Ensuring that disagreement relates only to principles and priorities, not personalities.

Respect for others. Board members are responsible for:

- Ensuring that everyone involved in synagogue life is treated with *kavod* (respect).
- Enabling those who are connected with synagogue life to reach their highest potential.
- Teaching that all are created *b'tzelem Elohim* (in the image of God) and that being a Jew is an honor and a privilege.
- Remembering and reminding others that the goal is unity, not uniformity.
- Ensuring that respect for boundaries, prerogatives, and expertise is the norm and that the position/office/calling of the clergy, professional staff, and lay leaders is worthy of respect.
- It was not with our fathers that Adonai made this covenant, but with us, the living, every one of us who is here today (Deuteronomy 5:3).

Board Self-government

When the board creates policies for others, it gives necessary guidance and then stops—leaving further decisions to the discretion of the people on the scene. When it creates policies for its own operation, there is no "other" to exercise discretion: the board takes complete responsibility for its own functioning, and it delegates only internally, to its own leaders. Consequently, this section of the policy book may go into considerably more detail than any other.

BOARD AGENDA

A board that does not take control of its agenda will soon find others more than willing to fill it with decisions that others could be making. A board's most important tasks—to discern the congregation's mission and calling, to make a few strategic choices about how the congregation will conduct its ministry, and to hold others accountable for overall results—are abstract and somewhat frustrating. Most people find it difficult to focus on them and easy to slip into the concrete world of management. A clear statement of how the board means to control its own agenda provides the basis for board members to call the group back onto task when its attention wanders.

EXAMPLE (CONSENT AGENDA)

Agenda team. The board empowers an agenda team, consisting of the board chair, senior minister, and clerk. The agenda team is responsible for the board packet, which shall contain all reports, the board agenda, and supporting materials. The packet as a whole may not exceed twenty-five pages, including a cover sheet containing a tentative agenda for the board meeting. The office shall e-mail the packet to each member of the board and senior staff no later than five days in advance of the board meeting.

Board reports. All reports must be e-mailed to the office at least a full week before the board meeting. All reports, including those of the senior clergy and treasurer, must be in writing and fewer than four pages in length. Late reports shall be held over for the following month's packet. The board shall not hear oral reports except when they are directly related to major items of board business. If a report contains a proposed board action, it must be stated in the form of a motion and placed at the top of the report.

The board agenda shall consist of a consent agenda and a discussion agenda. The consent agenda shall appear as a single item near the beginning of the board agenda, and shall include items requiring board action that the agenda team believes do not require discussion or debate. The discussion agenda for each meeting shall include not more than three major items, all of which relate directly to the board's discernment, strategy, and oversight roles.

The agenda team shall refuse any request for the board to act on a management item and refer such items to the appropriate ministry leader for decision. The agenda team may place a related policy item onto the consent or discussion agenda if appropriate.

BOARD COMMITTEES

Board committees are discussed in chapter 4. Because so many congregations are accustomed to using committees as an all-purpose organizational tool, it is important to make it clear exactly what committees the board intends to have and for what purposes.

EXAMPLE

The board shall appoint the following standing committees:

- The governance committee shall help the board to focus on its chosen role, to recruit and train board members, and to lead the annual board self-evaluation process.
- The finance committee shall assist the board in its oversight of the congregation's finances. It shall ensure that routine financial reports are clear and helpful, and coordinate the annual audit. From time to time, it shall hold educational sessions to ensure that board members have adequate understanding of the congregation's financial status and goals. The committee has no management authority, and shall not participate in day-to-day financial decision making.
- The personnel committee shall assist the board in developing personnel policies, ensuring compliance with applicable laws, and carrying out the staff grievance process as defined by these policies. The committee reports to the board, has no staff management authority, and shall not participate in day-to-day personnel decision making.

From time to time, the board shall appoint ad hoc committees and task forces to assist the board in its work of discernment, strategy, and oversight. Such committees and task forces shall receive a clear written charge that specifies the board's objectives, desired work products, and a time frame for completion of the task. Board committees shall not be used for open-ended management of programs or activities, which shall be delegated by policy, normally to the staff.

CONFLICTS OF INTEREST

The congregation's mission deserves each board member's loyalty. When what is best for the mission conflicts with a board member's personal interests or preferences, the member's duty is to act for the mission. A conflict of interest arises whenever a potential action of the board seems likely to benefit or harm a board member or a close relative. The clearest conflicts are financial—as, for instance, when the congregation buys something from a company owned by a board member—but there are subtler conflicts. For example, a board member might belong to the board of a preschool that rents space from a church, an art museum that bids on paintings at a synagogue fundraising auction, or a community center that competes for gifts from members of the congregation.

Because intertwined relationships are typical of congregations, it is not realistic to avoid all conflicts of interest, but the board can protect its members from criticism and embarrassment by having a clear policy for handling them. There are three levels of response to conflicts of interest: disclosure, recusal, and resignation. Mild conflicts of interest (for instance, when a board member's cousin holds stock in an office-supply chain) can be managed simply by disclosing them. If the remaining board members agree that the conflict is minor, the affected member can continue to participate in the decision. More serious conflicts—for instance, where a member's daughter is a candidate for a scholarship—require recusal: the member leaves the room and does not discuss or vote on that item. More serious conflicts of interest—for instance, if a board member is a contractor who wants to bid on a new building—involve such a pervasive division of loyalty that resignation is required. The choice of the level of response that fits a specific case is best made by board members who are not affected by the conflict.

It is a good idea to make disclosure of ongoing potential conflicts of interest an annual routine. This is a good occasion to note that conflicts of interest are inevitable. This acknowledgment makes it easier for members to disclose conflicts that arise later, when the board takes up an issue that affects them.

EXAMPLE

Board members shall carry out their duties with undivided loyalty to the congregation and its mission. A conflict of interest exists whenever a board member or a close relative of a board member has interests or duties that interfere with the board member's duty of loyalty. The conflicting interest may be financial, moral, political, theological, or otherwise.

Conflicts of interest arise when a board member:

- Stands to gain or lose because of a board action.
- Has a fiduciary duty or close personal or business relationship to any person or corporation that stands to gain or lose because of a board action. A board member who is an employee or close relative of an employee of the congregation always has a conflict of interest with respect to any board action affecting such employment.
- Holds a substantial property interest in a corporation or business, or serves as an officer or board member of another nonprofit organization that stands to gain or lose because of a board action.
- Cannot set aside his or her personal preferences as an individual consumer of the congregation's services to vote in behalf of the whole congregation and its mission.
- Faces any other situation that creates or appears to create divided or conflicting loyalties.

The board shall annually require its members to disclose in writing all existing or foreseeable conflicts of interest. Disclosure forms shall be kept by the board clerk and made available to any member of the congregation who requests them.

If an item of business arises in which any member suggests that a conflict of interest may exist, the affected member may withdraw or ask the board for guidance. In the latter case, the board (minus the affected parties) shall determine how to handle the situation. Depending on the seriousness of the conflict, possible responses include

- *Disclosure.* A supplemental disclosure form shall be filed by the affected member, who may then continue to participate and vote as usual.
- *Recusal.* The member shall disclose the conflict and withdraw from the meeting while the item is under discussion or voted on.
- *Resignation.* The member shall resign from the board.

The member with the potential conflict shall withdraw while the remaining board members determine whether a conflict exists and how it should be handled.

Anyone who exercises authority delegated by the board, including paid and unpaid staff members, is subject to the same standards of loyalty that apply to board members.

DISCIPLINE AND REMOVAL OF BOARD MEMBERS

A board has the right to discipline members who fail in their duties or disrupt the body's work, with a maximum punishment of expulsion. The bylaws or similar documents should address the process for removing board members from office. If the bylaws are silent, state law may provide for this serious but important means of self-protection. If there is any unclarity about the law, the board should consult with an attorney experienced in working with nonprofit corporations in its particular state before proceeding.

A policy on expulsion of board members needs to protect freedom of expression while preserving board discipline. Every board must write its own standards, so that new board members have fair notice of what is expected. A standard of conduct that is not generally enforced or observed cannot fairly be used to justify expelling a board member.

EXAMPLE

Before exercising its power under the bylaws to remove board members, the board shall notify the member in writing of its intent to do so and offer the member the opportunity for a hearing before the board. Pending a hearing, the board may suspend a board member's voting privileges without notice if necessary to protect individuals or the congregation from harm.

If a board member misses more than three meetings in a six-month period, the clerk shall automatically place the question of expulsion before the board. Other reasons for expulsion include, but are not limited to, serious violations of the board covenant or conflict-of-interest policy.

Discernment

Discernment includes all that a congregation does to discover and articulate its mission. Typical products of this work include mission and vision statements and a list of core values—all of which should be designed to last at least for several years.

Mission Statement
Who are we? What difference do we make, and for whom?

If your mission statement is adopted by the congregation, it does not belong among the board policies—though it may be convenient to include it at the front of the board policy book. If the mission statement is adopted by the board, it is a board policy (though it may seem odd to call it one), because it is meant to control many decisions over time. Mission statements also share with other policies a tendency to fade into the depths of a minute book and be forgotten. A board that seriously means to engage in discernment and planning should establish a regular routine of refreshing its plans. Putting those plans where the board must stumble over them while looking up board policies on building rentals is a good way to ensure that they will at least be seen.

Many congregations' mission statements read like catalogues—
they list all of the activities a church or synagogue of a given
denomination might engage in, with little sense of priority or
distinctiveness or forward motion. Such statements do no harm,
but they don't do much good either. The best mission statements
convey a sense of how this congregation in particular intends to
make a difference in the lives of people.

EXAMPLE

The mission of St. Peter's United Church of Christ [Carmel, In-
diana] is to carry the Word of God and teachings of Jesus Christ
to the greater community through creative ministries. We will
provide a place for individuals to organize and worship God. We
will provide ministries for individuals to grow as Christians. We
will develop lay leaders to create, design, and deliver new, exciting ministries. We will provide ministries to help others and share
God's love. We will continuously look to improve our programs
and offerings to those we serve.

EXAMPLE

The mission of Beth El Synagogue Talmud Torah [Omaha, Ne-
braska] is to teach our children the richness of Jewish life, help
them achieve positive Jewish identities, and encourage them to
actively participate in Jewish life.

Core Values
What principles do we intend to observe, no matter what?

In addition to its mission, each congregation has a set of core
values: principles it intends to observe in its organizational life.
Sometimes these values are so deeply embedded that it is difficult
to identify them until they are violated. The following examples
will give some sense of how widely congregational core values can
vary.

EXAMPLE (KALEO CHURCH, SAN DIEGO, CALIFORNIA)

For the church to remain socially relevant, we believe it is crucial to recognize, and be in contact with, popular thought. Fellowship of Kaleo from the beginning has emphasized four concepts, which we believe are grossly misunderstood in today's "popular mind." We believe it is crucial also for the church to not only recognize, but to understand, and be able to discuss and explain truthfully, these concepts. We refer to them as our Core Values.

- Meaning—God is eternal and therefore gives meaning to every age, culture, and worldview. For this reason, Kaleo seeks to continually understand cultural and worldview shifts to effectively minister to new generations.
- Beauty—God is beautiful, and his creation reflects his beauty. God created man and woman in his image and likeness to also create works of beauty. For this reason, Kaleo values the arts, expression, and creativity.
- Truth—God is True and has made his Truth known in his Word and the person of Jesus Christ. For this reason, Kaleo seeks to know, live, and proclaim Truth out of a love for God.
- Community—God exists in a perfect community of Father, Son, and Holy Spirit, and created men and women to also live in community. For this reason, Kaleo seeks to model deep and personal faith by serving others in a loving and authentic community.
- The Gospel—All four of these Core Values fit within the gospel. Simply, the gospel is the "good news" of God's redemption of mankind.

EXAMPLE (MCLEAN BIBLE CHURCH, MCLEAN, VA)

In order to accomplish our vision, McLean must be a unique kind of church—the kind of church that God can use to make a difference in Washington and beyond. Our Ten Core Values define us, guide us, and ensure that everything we do is aligned with our vision.

1. People matter to God—and to us (Luke 15).
2. The Gospel message transforms people's lives (2 Corinthians 5:17).
3. The goal of our ministry is to transform people into fully devoted followers of Christ (Matthew 28:18–20; Ephesians 4:11-16).
4. Ministry and evangelism must be carried out in a relevant way (1 Corinthians 9:22b).
5. People must be treated gently and respectfully (1 Peter 3:15).
6. People need to be connected to a caring community (Acts 4:34–35).
7. Every Christian has a God-given ministry (Ephesians 4:12).
8. Everything we do must be done with excellence (Colossians 3:23–24).
9. Our church must have an evangelistic impact on our community (Acts 6:7; 1 Thessalonians 1:8).
10. To accomplish our mission we must be willing to step out in visionary faith and take risks for God (Hebrews 11:6).

Open Questions

What are the unanswered questions we mean to reflect upon in the coming year?

Open questions, discussed in chapter 7, enable the board to invite the congregation to participate in discernment early in the process, before the board itself is ready to present plans or proposals. Open questions may address practical issues like a possible relocation, or they may inquire more deeply into the congregation's identity, purpose, and calling. It is better to have a short list of open questions (one, two, or three) than a long one.

EXAMPLES

- Shall we undertake an intentional effort to reach particular groups that we are not now reaching?
- What is our brand? How do we wish to be known by the community?
- How shall we ensure financial sustainability? What is the place or mission of this church in a new economic

situation?

- How shall we design experiences and services to meet a variety of spiritual and social needs while maintaining congregational unity?
- How shall we identify the needs of the people of the five hundred new homes in our community and determine if we should serve those needs?
- What presence will this congregation have outside our four walls (e.g., in our city and denominational community)?

Strategy

Deciding when to undertake a capital campaign, setting the overall operating budget, and approving the hiring or dismissal of principal staff members—all these are strategic, "macro-management" decisions, appropriate for the board to make directly if it chooses to. Exactly how detailed the board's strategic policies will be depends partly on its policies on delegation, found under "management," below. Any board should hit the high spots. At any time, a member of the staff or congregation should know (or be able to find out) what major projects the board has chosen for the long and the short term.

Strategic Plan
What major choices have we made about how we will fulfill our mission?

A strategic plan falls between the congregation's mission statement, which attempts to capture its basic, lasting purpose—and its vision of ministry, which details its priorities for the next year or two. A strategic plan indicates the major means by which the congregation will fulfill its mission over a five- to ten-year span of time. It includes plans for program and membership development, staffing, and capital-development steps, like building programs and endowment funds. Many alternative strategies could be faithful to the mission; through a process of strategic planning, the congregation chooses one set of strategies it plans to stick with.

Typically a strategic plan takes a year or more to create, and may run several or many pages. Only a part of the full strategic plan—the summary statement of major strategic choices—belongs in the board policy book.

In congregations that wish to observe the distinction between governance and ministry as presented in this book, a strategic planning team has two customers. If the plan includes a revised mission statement, guidance for board policies, governance-change proposals, or overall strategic goals, its customer is the board or congregation. To the extent that it includes detailed program ideas, timelines, budgets, and specific staffing changes, its customer is the staff in its role as ministry decision maker.

EXAMPLE (CENTENARY UMC, WINSTON-SALEM, NC)

- *Enlist.* Centenary will unlock and open our doors wide, and actively welcome and involve people in the Christian community of Centenary United Methodist Church.
- *Equip.* Centenary will nurture the congregation and community with authentic ministries that are relevant, innovative, and focused on spiritual development of our members from cradle to grave. We seek to be a community of lifelong disciples, and therefore lifelong learners, who exemplify and uphold our United Methodist tradition.
- *Deploy.* Centenary will inspire and excite our church family to reach out and actively share the gift of Christian discipleship in love and service, through more focused ministries that impact our congregation and neighbors in our downtown community.

Vision of Ministry
In what new and different ways will we transform lives in the next three to five years?

The vision of ministry is a short list of the board's top priorities, with enough detail to make it possible for the board to hold the staff accountable, but not so much that the board invades the realm of management. The list is revised and updated or replaced annually at the board planning retreat.

EXAMPLE

- In order to support growth, we will add a second weekly worship service; make adjustments in staffing, education, program, and budget; and plan for enlarging the program wing of the church.
- As a community of lifelong learners with a message of love and unity amid diversity, we will increase the number of participants in our life-span learning program by 20 percent through greater outreach to the wider community.
- To promote intimate caring and sharing, deepening relationships, and expanded self-awareness, we will support and encourage expansion of the Small Group Ministry Program to twenty groups.

Management

Strong boards do not manage; they govern. But to keep focus on governance, they need policies that delegate management decisions to others. Policies on management delegate parts of the board's power and authority to others. Delegation is essential if the board is to focus on its core roles of discernment, strategy, and oversight. Most practical decisions can safely be made away from the board table, provided that the board adopts clear and limited delegation policies, gives the decision maker guidance as to the larger goals to be achieved, and establishes effective ways to monitor progress and evaluate results. Given such a structure of policy, even boards that otherwise might want to weigh in every month can feel more comfortable delegating more authority and exercising oversight on a less frequent basis.

Effective delegation requires that the board keep three elements in proper balance: authority, accountability, and guidance. If any one of these is missing or out of proportion, the board is likely to find decisions it thought it had delegated back on its agenda until it corrects the situation.

Delegation to the Staff

Most operational details can be delegated to the staff, as discussed in chapter 7. In most nonprofits, the head of staff is an executive director or chief executive officer, who in turn delegates to other members of the staff. Some congregations follow this example, while others vest management authority in a leadership team.

GLOBAL DELEGATION

The policy on global delegation ensures that when unanticipated questions come up, there will always be a way to decide them short of bringing them automatically to the board. In place of a "zero-based" system of delegation, the global delegation policy delegates *everything* about management to the head of staff. Other policies then limit and constrain the delegated power to whatever extent the board thinks necessary.

> EXAMPLE
>
> The head of staff (or leadership team) shall lead and direct the spiritual, programmatic, and administrative work of the church, and is hereby delegated authority and responsibility to make all operational decisions, adopt administrative policies, and allocate congregational resources except as specifically limited by these policies.

> EXAMPLE
>
> The head of staff shall lead and direct the spiritual, programmatic, and administrative work of the church in concert with the ministry council, consisting of the senior staff and ministry team leaders, appointed by the head of staff with the approval of the board. The head of staff shall consult with the ministry council and seek

its support before making important operational decisions. The ministry council shall have an opportunity to review and endorse the annual budget before the head of staff presents it to the board. The board hereby empowers the head of staff to take any action not specifically prohibited or reserved to others by these policies.

STAFF STRUCTURE

The board should define the structure of the top-level staff, making it clear who is responsible for staff performance and provides the primary communication link between the staff and board. This is the place to state who is the head of staff and what that role entails. If a team serves as head of staff, this is the place to answer questions about succession, tie-breaking, and conflict management within the team. Options for staff structure are discussed in chapter 7, pp. 136–142.

EXAMPLE

The senior minister shall serve as head of staff and be responsible for maintaining a productive and effective staff team, for ensuring that its efforts are directed toward fulfilling the congregation's mission and vision of ministry, and for staff compliance with all board policies.

The board shall designate certain staff positions as "senior" (currently ———, ——— , and ———). The senior staff team shall share responsibility with the head of staff for the operational leadership.

Delegation to Others

As discussed in chapter 3, it sometimes makes sense, especially in larger congregations, to place certain functions outside the regular ministry leadership structure. A day school and an endowment committee are common examples.

EXAMPLE

The board shall appoint an endowment committee, which shall

have charge of all funds given with the restriction that income only may be used. In addition, the board may designate other donations as "voluntarily restricted" so that they can be treated as permanent funds until the board removes the designation. The endowment committee shall have the power to engage, at the expense of the endowment funds, investment advisors and fund managers.

- Endowment funds shall be invested with the goal of achieving, over the long run, a total return of 4 percent, plus the rate of inflation as measured by the Consumer Price Index, through a diversified portfolio limited to investments commonly utilized by charitable endowments with similar goals.
- Endowment funds shall be invested with the additional goal of avoiding investments in companies that violate our moral values, and of promoting responsible corporate behavior. To achieve this goal, the endowment committee shall adopt a written policy on socially responsible investing.
- Each year on September 30, the market value of each endowment fund shall be recorded. The total amount transferred for current use each year shall not exceed 4 percent of the average of the market value for the last three years.

EXAMPLE

The board shall appoint a school committee to govern the Hilltop Nursery School as a service of the congregation to the community. The purpose of the HNS is to provide excellent preschool education to an economically and ethnically diverse community of students.

- The school committee shall adopt policies to ensure the school's compliance with applicable laws and to limit the congregation's liability and other risks. The committee shall report promptly to the board any significant changes to school policy, risks, or problems.
- The school committee shall recommend a school director for appointment by the board.
- The school director and committee shall propose annual goals for board approval.
- The school committee shall annually evaluate the director's

performance and report the results to the board.

- As part of the annual budget process, the head of staff shall estimate the fair market value of building space and other benefits provided to the school by the congregation. The budget shall provide for an internal transfer of funds from the school account to the operating fund in recognition of this value.

Care for People

The board's duty of care requires that it ensure the personal safety of all who come under the congregation's umbrella. As with other operational matters, the most effective way for the board to fulfill this duty is to state clearly what it expects of the ministry leadership. Individual board members who have talents to offer can doff their board hats temporarily and join the staff as volunteers.

EXAMPLE

The head of staff shall be responsible for taking care to prevent harm to the members and guests who take part in congregational activities or use the property, and shall have the power to take all necessary steps to deal with situations where such persons are at risk.

Health and safety. The head of staff shall ensure that all facilities are maintained in a safe, sanitary, and secure condition, that required licenses and inspections are kept up to date, and that problems are corrected promptly. A paid or unpaid staff member shall be designated as the health and safety officer responsible for addressing health and safety issues.

- *Emergency planning.* The head of staff shall maintain a written plan for responding to medical emergencies, fire, toxic conditions, weather problems, threatening communications, power outages, natural disasters, and other circumstances that create or threaten dangerous conditions. A paid or unpaid staff member shall be designated as the emergency planning officer responsible for preparing emergency-response procedures and conducting drills and training as required.
- *Sexual harassment.* Employees, volunteers, and agents of

the congregation are prohibited from acts of sexual harassment against any member or participant in congregational activities or any employee or applicant for employment. In response to violations of this policy, the head of staff or board shall, as necessary, take disciplinary action, which may include termination of employment or membership or exclusion from congregational property and programs.

- *Child protection.* Because of our special responsibility for children and youth in the congregation's care, the head of staff shall establish clear, written procedures for the selection, training, and supervision of all paid and unpaid staff who work with persons age eighteen and younger.

Nondiscrimination. No one acting for the congregation shall discriminate because of race, color, age, sex, marital status, sexual orientation, disability, national origin or ancestry, economic status, union membership, or political affiliation. Employment shall be based solely on merit and qualification. Religious opinions and affiliation may be considered only in the case of paid or unpaid staff positions that include religious teaching or worship leadership.

Universal access. The congregation intends to make its premises and activities accessible to persons with the widest possible variety of disabilities. To this end it will meet and exceed all legal requirements, and engage in continual examination of its properties, practices, and attitudes.

Care for Staff

Boards are often reluctant to delegate decisions about personnel and money. Their concerns are understandable, but it is not practical for a board to make all such decisions directly. The most effective way for the board to ensure that important decisions are made as it would wish is to create policies that guide and circumscribe the actions of the staff.

EXAMPLE

The head of staff shall be responsible for maintaining a productive and effective staff team, for ensuring that its efforts are directed toward fulfilling the congregation's mission and vision of ministry, and for compliance by the staff with all board policies.

- Compensation for congregation staff shall be competitive with comparable positions in local or denominational markets, and will comply with guidelines for fair compensation as approved by [the denomination].
- All staff members working more than twenty hours per week shall receive, after completing a six-month probationary period, a uniform benefits package including health insurance and retirement plan contributions.
- Prior to creating a new staff position or seeking applicants to fill a staff vacancy, the head of staff shall consult with the board personnel committee, which shall assist in preparing contracts and terms of offer. The head of staff shall report to and consult with the board prior to making a decision to proceed.
- Prior to a search for a senior staff member, the head of staff shall appoint a search committee, which shall consult widely to determine the congregation's needs and preferences. The head of staff shall work with the search committee to identify and evaluate candidates, and shall consult with them and with continuing senior staff members before making a hiring decision.
- Prior to discharging a staff member, the head of staff shall consult with the personnel committee to ensure that the proposed decision adheres to accepted personnel practices and complies with applicable laws, bylaws, and board policies.
- The head of staff shall be responsible for maintaining an up-to-date personnel manual covering matters not specifically addressed in these board policies, as required to ensure that the church complies with legal requirements and denominational norms for employment practices.

Care for Resources

Whether the person who manages the congregation's finances is paid or unpaid, he or she is part of the staff, acting with power delegated by the board. Because of the potential for misconduct, the board needs to create a thorough framework of guidance and accountability in the area of finance. Well-written financial policies protect the congregation's funds from misuse or misappropriation, and protect financial managers from false accusations of misconduct.

EXAMPLE

The head of staff, together with senior staff members in their areas of responsibility, shall be responsible for day-to-day fiscal decisions. The head of staff may not:

- Exceed the total budgeted spending for the year.
- Exceed budgeted spending in any top-level budget category by more than $10,000.
- Incur new debt on behalf of the church. The board may approve credit cards, lines of credit, or other borrowing in advance.
- Buy or sell real estate, or invest in securities other than bank deposits or high-quality money market funds.
- Accept any gift that is restricted by the donor as to use or purpose. The board may approve restricted donations for specific purposes by approving in advance the creation of a designated fund or wish list.
- Use donor-restricted funds in violation of donor restrictions and trust provisions.
- Jeopardize the congregation's tax-exempt status under local, state, or federal law.
- Change the compensation of any staff position, or the church's policy on compensation and benefits.

EXAMPLE

The head of staff shall be responsible for preventing harm to the congregation's reputation or assets. The board treasurer will work with the staff to develop policies and practices designed to prevent such harm, and report promptly to the board on any significant shortcomings in their implementation.

- *Financial controls.* Written procedures shall govern the handling of receipts, access to cash and bank balances, approval of expenditures, payment of invoices and other obligations, and management of invested funds. Two unrelated persons shall maintain joint control of all cash until it is deposited. Two unrelated persons shall approve all disbursements. The functions of record keeping, bank reconciliation, and cash disbursements shall be under the control of three unrelated persons.
- *Accounting.* The congregation's financial accounts shall follow generally accepted accounting practices to the extent that those practices are usually followed by congregations of our size. Particular care shall be taken to distinguish donor-restricted, temporarily restricted, voluntarily restricted, and unrestricted funds.
- *Document retention.* Written procedures shall govern the retention and destruction of documents, giving definite retention periods for classes of financial, business, pastoral, personnel, and corporate records in both paper and electronic forms.
- *Insurance.* The congregation shall maintain adequate insurance to protect against property losses and liability for injuries to others. The board shall annually review and approve the insurance coverage.

Powers Reserved to the Board

Most boards choose to keep certain matters clearly in their own court, even at the risk of multiplying the number of small items they must deal with. Some denominations require the governing board to act on certain matters (the session of a Presbyterian church, for instance, must approve new members), in which case there is no need for a board policy saying the same thing. But there may be other matters a board wishes not to delegate. If it has adopted a global delegation policy (see above) it must then explicitly reserve such matters to itself.

EXAMPLES

- The board reserves to itself the power to affiliate the congregation with other organizations, and to take related actions such as setting contribution levels, appointing delegates, and voting in elections of affiliated bodies.
- The board reserves to itself the power to commit the congregation to positions on public or political questions. This provision shall not limit the right of clergy or lay leaders to express personal opinions and to identify themselves by their positions in the congregation.

Oversight

The board's duty of care requires it to ensure that the congregation's human and material resources are used for the benefit of its mission. The board fulfills this duty both negatively, by preventing theft and loss of resources, and positively, by requiring that the ministry be active, forward-looking, and appropriately bold. To fulfill this responsibility the board needs to say what it wants (through policies on discernment and strategy) and whom it will empower to lead (through policies on delegation). Oversight policies complete this picture by establishing a plan for monitoring and evaluating that work so staff and lay program leaders are accountable, and so that the congregation learns from its experience.

A board that spends too much time checking up on its staff might just as well not delegate in the first place; by second-guessing the decisions of its staff, it trains staff members to be overcautious. Policies on oversight set performance and reporting standards for all who work in the congregation's name, and establish annual routines for planned evaluation by the board of staff performance.

Monitoring

Effective oversight requires policies that set up regular routines so that the board can monitor the work and evaluate results. Monitoring needs to be focused if it is to mean anything: flooding board members with irrelevant paper or tedious oral reports actually reduces their awareness of how the congregation's ministry is or is not following the guidelines it has laid down or rising to the goals it has set.

EXAMPLE

The staff, ministry teams, committees, and board of trustees shall engage in a continual process of monitoring and evaluation. The purposes to be accomplished through monitoring and evaluation are to foster excellence in ministry work by encouraging open communication and regular feedback among all whose work contributes to achieving the church's mission, to help the church to focus on its goals as adopted by the board, and to ensure that all church leaders adhere closely to board policies.

The head of staff shall be responsible for regular written reports from the staff to the board. Reports shall focus on progress on priorities, as set by the board through the annual vision of ministry, and on compliance with board policy.

- Financial reports shall show overall financial performance compared to budget and highlight significant financial or operational issues. These reports shall be e-mailed to board members in advance of each monthly meeting, but shall not normally be a subject of board discussion except when they require board action or raise issues of compliance with board policy. Financial statements shall be filed and made available to any congregation member who wishes to examine them.
- The board shall call upon the staff on a planned basis through the year to report more fully on the church's work in a given area, and to contribute expertise, information, and leadership. The purpose of these reports is to support the board's learning and reflection on major areas of the church's mission, such as worship, religious education, social justice, membership development, and stewardship of congregational property and wealth.
- From time to time, the board may inquire into specific questions of policy compliance, organizational concerns, or other serious issues by appointing a committee or outside

consultant to assess some aspect of church program or organizational functioning.

- Annually, the treasurer shall engage a qualified professional to conduct an audit of the church's financial records and report in writing to the board.

Evaluation

Goal setting and evaluation, as discussed in chapter 7, are at the heart of effective partnership between the leaders of governance and ministry. A simple policy is best—elaborate designs are best left to be created year by year, lest high ambitions lead to giving up entirely. In some years, a short evaluation session is more than enough.

The board does not need to adopt policies about the evaluation of staff members other than those who report directly to the board. Where that person is a clergy leader, it is important to provide a more widely inclusive review process—in the example, I suggest once every three years—to recognize that the total job of a minister or rabbi includes much more than simply being CEO.

EXAMPLE

- *Program evaluation.* Each spring, as part of the creation of the vision of ministry, the head of staff and board shall together review their mutual progress in light of the prior year's vision of ministry and related goals.
- *Board and head of staff evaluation.* At least once a year, board members and the head of staff shall evaluate their own and one another's contributions to the church's mission.
- *Staff evaluations.* The senior staff shall be responsible for creating and carrying out an annual cycle of evaluation that shall produce, at minimum, a written evaluation of each staff member by his or her supervisor, which shall be available for inspection by the board or its authorized representatives. The primary purpose of staff and program team evaluation is to recognize achievement, build morale, and enhance communication and working relationships.

- *Clergy leader's triennial performance review.* Every three years, the board and clergy leader shall together appoint a triennial review committee of three persons held in high esteem by the congregation and mutually acceptable to the board and clergy leader. The committee shall facilitate a performance review of the clergy leader's performance, gathering data from the congregation and other sources, and producing a written report. The task force report, together with a written response from the clergy leader, shall be published to the congregation. The goals of the triennial performance review are to call the congregation's attention to the mutual, relational nature of ministry and the respective responsibilities of all who contribute to its success; to assist the clergy leader to remain motivated, creative, and flexible; and to equip the clergy leader and board to correct any problems and maintain an effective partnership in the future.